Butterfly Words
Relationships: A Psychiatrist's Narrative

Butterfly Words
Relationships: A Psychiatrist's Narrative

By Daniel Rosen

Translations from French and Hebrew by the author

International Psychoanalytic Books (IPBooks)
New York • https://ipbooks.net

© 2019 by Daniel Rosen.

International Psychoanalytic Books (IPBooks)
Queens, NY 11102
Online at: https://ipbooks.net

All rights reserved. No part of this book may be used or reproduced in any manner whatsoever including Internet usage, without written permission of the author, except in the case of brief quotations embodied in critical articles and reviews.

Cover page photo: *Reflections* by Daniel Rosen, 2007.

ISBN: 978-1-949093-03-2

Foreword 1-2

Introduction 3-11

1 Paris 13
The melody   15-17
The device   19-25
The revolt   27-28
Lena   29-30

2 New in America 31
New in town   33-34
In a cloud of smoke   35-38
Let's go, children   39-41
The last leaf   42-43
Words' cemetery   45
A pink short coat   47-48
We will be back   49-50

3 Jerusalem 51
Missing Jerusalem   53-55
Days of Awe - High Holidays   57-61
In the center   63-64
Hitnatkut (A house destroyed) *(in Hebrew and English)*   65-66
Insha'Allah (God willing)   67-68
Israeli fashion   69

4 Longing for Jerusalem 71
In the streets of Jerusalem   73
Trilogy   75
A new stone   77
I looked   79

5 New York 86

Stones 83
As before 85-86
Till the end 87
The sparks between us 89
Butterfly words 91
Opera 93
Beth 95-96
Beth II 97
Cholent 99
Sparks 101
Shhh... 103
Ice breaker 105
Singing Questions 107-109
Last smile 111
That smile again 113-114
The Mirabeau Bridge *(in French and English)* 115
Blushing dress 117
Fire 119
A rose and a fox *(in French and English)* 121
People and places 123
Third wish 125
After the *chag* 127
Share a poem 129
Contained fire 131-132
Mechitza 133
Without love 135
Avi *(in French and English)* 137

6 Relationships: A psychiatrist's narrative 139-147

7 Original writings in French & Hebrew 149-186

8 Just a brunch 187-206
A psychiatrist's narrative
The question 189-190
The sacrifice of Sarah 191-193
I swear! I swear! I swear! 194
The sacrifice of Tamás 195-201
The list 202-205
The brunch 206

9 The oldnew bracelet 207-263
Relationship with the ancestors
Le nouveau-vieux bracelet (*in French*) 209-226
The platter 227-232
The bracelet 233-243
Nouna 245-255
Forever ephemeral 257
La mêlée (*in French*) 261
The scrum 263

Afterword 265-270

About the author 271

Foreword

The words collected here were written because they were a necessity at the time. For each occasion, they fulfilled a specific and sometimes different purpose: reflect on a relationship, engage in a new one, or mourn a lost one. Sometime the necessity was out of duty towards those who were left behind, or to share a happy or sad experience, or trying to master and anticipate those experiences. Relationships are at the core of these writings. The relationships could be at the individual level, familial, communal, at a national level or even broader. They could also involve multiple levels. Over many years, these writings were stored as we collect memories, as souvenirs collect dust. Until, one day, I started dusting off those real or imagined memories. They were gathered and they met in this collection. And then, they started talking to each other, communicating without any control, like a Golem escaping his creator.

I am so grateful to William S. Cohen for catching these internal conversations and disclosing meanings and connections I could not even fathom. His insights are recorded in the introduction. I have been asked: "Who is this William S. Cohen who seems to know you so well?" Yes, he has been with me all these years, a devoted observer, sometimes detached, sometimes ironic. I have chosen his pen name to analyze the writings the way he would, just as an impartial critic looks into a foreign text.

Special thanks to Renée Passy Alfandary and Adrian P Gonzalez M, each of whom helped translate here an early work. Another special thank-you to Isabelle Tardé who reviewed the writings in French. I thank also my friends and all the involuntary participants or recipients of those poems and stories. I thank all those who inspired me, as I thank the muses; the amused muses who played with me and wrote these words.

Daniel Rosen

Introduction

By William S. Cohen

This collection of writings covers a varied range of emotions across different settings over several decades. The initial poem of the New York chapter, **Stones**, sets the stage for the following poems by pretending an apparent dichotomy between hope and despair, love and death. Past relationships are a weight, like the stones used in traditional Jewish burials, but also a source of comfort. The dark image of being buried by the stones/relationships/poems is only partially mitigated by the more hopeful second stanza. However, the last line of the poem "One last time" suggests that the comfort given by the precious stones is the ultimate one before the inevitable end. In **As before**, the poem itself is a source of comfort and a reminder of the precious memories remaining after a relationship has receded. The theme of a bittersweet end is repeated in **Till the end**, where the "epilogue of your breath" refers to the foreshadowed death of the loved one. The next poem, **The sparks between us**, while still bittersweet, is somewhat more hopeful as it seems to assume a continuous cycle and recycling of divine sparks present during the first encounter and returning to their source after death.

The next poem, **Butterfly words**, is clearly in a more playful register than the others. Here, the author plays with words (as if words were a ball to play with) combining wordplay in three languages. In French *mots de tête* (words of the head) is pronounced like *maux de tête* (headaches). In this poem it is associated with *mots d'esprit* (words of the mind) which could also mean wordplay; and this is therefore a wordplay with the word "wordplay." The Hebrew for "words" is *milim*. It is associated with the question from Pirkei Avot: *mi li*, "Who is for me?" [1]

The love poem ***In the street of Jerusalem*** has a life of its own, symbolizing the desired relationship and closeness to the body of the loved one, in an airy and sensual contact to rhythm of the legs. ***Trilogy***, as in ***People and places***—and to a certain extent in ***Missing Jerusalem***—exposes the competing relationships between Paris, New York and Jerusalem; here the cities are viewed as lovers. Even if Manhattan is preferred over Paris, the poem undercuts that choice by using the neologism "Manhattanien," which sounds more like *parisien* (the French word for "Parisian"), instead of the more accepted word "Manhattanite."

In ***A new stone***, the stone symbolizes the home/Temple, and the kiss is also devotional. As in ***Beth***, ***Beth II*** and ***Hitnatkut (A house destroyed)***, the family home and God's Temple are two enmeshed concepts. Both are called *bayit* in Hebrew (pronounced "Beit" when in a construct state, close to the English name "Beth"). The repetition/translation in Hebrew of the words "second home" in ***Beth II*** changes the association in English from a second home to the second Jerusalem Temple, called *beit sheni*—literally "second home"—which also happens to also be the title of the poem; ostensibly the second poem about a woman called Beth, but really about building a family home as a rebuilt second Temple.

In ***Hitnatkut (A house destroyed)***, the poem describes the spiritual isolation from God/Jerusalem, resulting from a broken home (or a home broken). This contrasts and mirrors the English poem ***Missing Jerusalem***. The personal and familial struggle is kept in synch with the collective experience

---

[1] He used to say: "If I am not for myself, who will be for me? And if I am only for myself, what am I? And if not now, when?" *Pirkei Avot (1:14)*

of redemption and exile. This poem could resonate on a communal level with the experience of family homes, along with their local synagogue, being physically broken during the disengagement (*"Hitnatkut"* in Hebrew) when those living in the Jewish settlements in Gaza were expelled by Jerusalem's Sharon government in August 2005. It could also resonate on a family level with a broken home, symbolically destroyed when a couple separates. The home/Temple symbols are merged in both examples. The English version of the title, translated by the author himself, points to the first interpretation; while the original Hebrew title, *hurban habayit*, is an expression commonly used for the past destructions of the Jerusalem Temple and does not refer explicitly to the *Hitnatkut*.

In a paradoxical way, the Hebrew poem **Hitnatkut (A house destroyed)**, by nature of its being in Hebrew and following the Jewish texts and symbols, expresses a closeness and longing (or a rejection and ambivalence) not matched in the English of **Missing Jerusalem**. The Hebrew text starts almost like a *kinnah* (lamentation) recited during the fast of Tisha B'Av (commemorating the destructions of the temple in Jerusalem), but seems to also reflect an emotional disengagement (*hitnatkut*) and distancing like in **In the center**. The motif of the children of Jerusalem overlaps the collective/Jerusalem and the individual/familial. The symbol of children filling the cracks of the Jerusalem's wall is seen in both poems, **Hitnatkut** and **Missing Jerusalem**. The children motif is again poignant in **Hitnatkut** with: "Leave my tongue in my palate (palate=*bekhiki*) / Leave my children in my bosom (bosom=*bekheki*)" where the children are associated with the tongue (a body part which cannot be detached), with the rich untranslatable internal rhyme *bekhiki-bekheki* בְּחִכִּי-בְּחֵיקִי (palate-bosom).

In this poem, symbols of blessing are repeatedly turned into symbols of desolation and curses. The next line " אֶת תַּעֲנָבַי

"שְׁנָתִי בְּעֵינַי" (Leave my sleep in my eyes) alludes to Jacob and his sleeplessness while guarding Lavan's sheep; an image which was turned into a morning blessing by the Jewish prayer book, where God is thanked for removing the sleep from our eyes and therefore reviving us from the "small death" caused by sleep. This despairing line turns the blessing upside down. On one hand, it could be seen as a request for more sleep to repair a night of insomnia caused by turmoil, but it may alternately allude to an unspoken death wish and curse. The curse can also be seen earlier in the line "רִמּוֹנֵינוּ בְּלִי גַרְעִינִים" (Our pomegranates, without seeds). What is left of a pomegranate if the seeds are absent? The lack of seeds represents the guilty absence of good deeds, an inversion of the well-known blessing recited on the Jewish New Year ("May our merits be as abundant as the pomegranate's seeds").

The original biblical sentence of "אִם אֶשְׁכָּחֵךְ יְרוּשָׁלָיִם" (If I forget you, Jerusalem, *Psalm 137:5-6*) is also turned upside down, from an enthusiastic vow of being close to Jerusalem, to the rejection of a plain curse with no spiritual redemption. Rabbi Elazar HaKalir (c. 570 – c. 640), in a *kinnah* recited on Tisha B'Av, also uses this verse as an image of curse and destruction: "If [it could happen that] the tongue of the nursing baby would adhere to its palate through unmitigated thirst— alas unto me!" (אם תדבק לשון יונק לחיך בצמאון צחיחים, אללי לי)[2].

Even in its ambivalence and its guilty rejection of the spiritual as represented by Jerusalem, the Hebrew poem/*kinnah* is imbued with the same connection (between the particular and the collective) as the English poem, ***Missing Jerusalem***, if not more.

---

[2] For a translation of this entire *kinnah*, see: http://www.beureihatefila.com/files/Sample_of_Translated_Kinos.pdf, page 10.

The influence of the Hebrew prayer book and Hebrew poetry can also be seen in *I looked*. The first part of the second stanza, "Here I am/Where the West ends/And my heart is in the East" alludes to a well-known poem by Yehuda Halevi (1075-1141) "My heart is in the east, and I am at the end of the west." The second part of the stanza refers to the East, here associated with Jerusalem, "Where a new light/Will shine over Zion"; like the Hebrew morning blessing: "A new light will shine over Zion, and may we all be worthy soon to enjoy its brightness."

A similar theme—associating interpersonal relationships with the communal experience of exile (the night) and redemption (the day of Shabbat)—is playfully used in ***Cholent***, the name of a traditional Jewish stew, usually simmered overnight on Friday night for the *Shabbat* meal the next day.

In ***Words' cemetery***, words again take a life of their own, symbolizing a now-dead relationship, while in ***Butterfly words***, they symbolize the emergence of a new one. Taken together, those two poems about love and death are reminiscent of the first poem, ***Stones***, where the words in the poems also symbolize relationships.

Some writings have a playful quality, as in ***Ice breaker***, ***Singing questions, That smile again, Fire***, and ***Third wish***. They are also sometimes self-deprecating, like ***Opera*** and ***Last smile***, or irreverent, like ***Sparks***, where the (holy?) sparks "niche on your uncovered knees atop a high stool"; or they are sexy, as are ***Blushing dress*** and ***Israeli fashion***. In that last poem, the two principal characters—the woman walking in the street and the person following her—are never mentioned. The woman's clothes and accessories are also characters, in relationship with each other through an impersonal mathematic formula. This detached and almost scientific description obscures its voyeuristic aspect and accentuates the comical incongruence of a fashion conscious

Israeli woman required to carry her military gun at all times, even while wearing sexy and unpractical civilian clothes. Similarly, in **The device,** at the end of the peripheral narrative (in italics) the legs of the desk and the back of the chair surrounding the receptionist are described in minute detail, omitting any description of the woman herself. In that short story, women are also absent from the central narrative (in bold) although their existence is implied (lipstick, perfume, perfume shop…). Relationships and women are central to the parallel and intertwined "commentary," which lacks the yearning for spirituality seen in some of the later writings. Here the clergy of two religions strike an irreverent deal between themselves, at the expense of both God and a dying man. The outside narrative is displayed in the style of a religious Talmudic commentary of the core text, as if human relationships were still a holy subject of discussion and attention, even when God is absent or silent.

In **Le pont Mirabeau**, the concept of bridge is itself a bridge between the secular (with a reference to Guillaume Apollinaire)[3], and the holy (with a reference to Rabbi Nachman of Bratslav)[4]. Similarly, we saw previously the concept of house, merging the profane house with its holy counterpart. This short poem is the only one rhyming in French, and has the following rhythm in French, if we count the number of syllables: 8-[4;3]-8-3.

In **A rose and a fox**, the original French version of the poem also has an interesting rhythm, lost in the English translation: (if we count *et un* as one syllable before *éléphant*) 3/7-7-7/5/7-7-8-8/5/7-8-7/7.

The three poems, **Share a poem**, **Contained Fire** and **Mechitza**, all explore the conflict between the hidden and

---

[3] http://www.writing.upenn.edu/library/Apollinaire_Mirabeau.html
[4] http://www.zemirotdatabase.org/view_song.php?id=220#rec

the revealed, between yearning for a new relationship and dreading the first real encounter that could destroy the dream. **Mechitza** concludes with a most daring mystical imagery, repeated quite innocently every Friday night when welcoming the *Shabbat*. The literal and crude English translation of the well-known Hebrew poem *Lechah Dodi* highlights the almost obscene experience of the mystic, transposing a physical sexual relationship between the bride and groom into a mystical relationship with God: "May your God rejoice/On you/Like a groom would/On his bride." Usually, translations say "with" or "over" his bride. The traditional blessing during the Jewish marriage does not dare to venture that far, and asks more modestly in a blessing that God rejoices in the groom *with* his bride (not *on* her).

The last poem, **Avi**, takes the counterpoint of Jacques Prévert's *Déjeuner du matin*[5] while also mirroring it. In **Avi**, the child doesn't talk either; nevertheless he interacts by looking at the narrator. The punch line "I put my hand over my eyes /And I cried" is similar in both poems. However, while in *Déjeuner du matin* it is a cry of distress, in **Avi** it is a cry of deep inner joy and emotional surprise at the gesture of a small boy who offers his most precious treasure, a box full of sand. The fundamental optimism of this poem contrasts with its counterpart from Prévert, and is also present in a poem about a lost relationship, **Without love**. Even that darkest poem retains in the last line the fond memory of the past love, like the precious diamond of the initial poem, **Stones**.

A different theme emerges from the older writings: A stranger observes people in a group and is progressively drawn emotionally to participate and connect with the group, while retaining some distance or discomfort: the burning wallet in **The melody**, and the amused enthusiasm in **Let's**

---

5 http://lyricstranslate.com/en/déjeuner-du-matin-breakfast.html

go children. The group can also be virtual, like former guests of a romantic inn (***We will be back***).

In ***The melody***, the observer becomes the messenger restoring the soul of a song for the Hasidim he visits in search of an authentic melody. As in *Transmigration of a Melody* by I. L. Peretz (1852-1915)[6], the Hasidic song is seen as having a soul returned in full force to its original location after having traveled back and forth to a new world. The messenger realizes that the treasure he was looking for across the Iron Curtain, the soul of an authentic Hasidic melody, was already within him.

In ***Days of Awe—High Holidays***, the 30th anniversary of the Yom Kippur war is experienced with a mixture of anxiety about the possibility of renewed war and excitement about an Israel worth surviving because of the kindness of its residents. Here, the new immigrant is drawn into an endless cycle of relationships, of receiving and giving, leading him to integrate with the residents of Jerusalem. Amos Oz, in *A Tale of Love and Darkness*, describes how simple day-to-day decisions—such as how much cheese to buy from Jewish or Arab farmers—could have existential repercussions for the Jewish people at the time of the birth of Israel. More than 50 years later, in ***Days of Awe***, the simple act of helping someone to go to a post office is still experienced not merely as an act of collective responsibility, but as an act of survival. This exaltation of and closeness with Israel, also found with the yearning toward Jerusalem in ***Insh'Allah***, contrasts with the distancing of next letter, ***In the center***, and in the Hebrew poem ***Hitnatkut (A house destroyed)***.

In the beginning of ***In a cloud of smoke***, the observer feels distant from the group, with the "absurd vision of himself

---

[6] See English translation from the original Yiddish:
https://archive.org/stream/nybc209367/nybc209367_djvu.txt

elbow to elbow with strangers". However, at the end, his emotional involvement is deep with the implied association of the mourning ritual for veterans with the martyrdom of Rabbi Haninah ben Teradion by the Romans, as recorded in the Babylonian Talmud (*Avodah Zarah*, 18a). While being torched alive while wrapped in a Torah scroll, the Rabbi said famously: "I see the parchment being consumed but the letters are flying off and they remain." The precious testimonies of the veterans are associated with the holy writings of the Torah. Both burnings are sacrilegious; however the spirits of the Torah scroll and of the veterans' letters escaped, just as the spirits of the Holocaust victims must have escaped their burning bodies in the crematorium. The ritual engages the observer by bringing up a personal loss related the Holocaust. The Holocaust is also in the background of **New in town**, **Days of Awe—High Holidays**, and **Let's go children**, and is implied in **The melody**.

Taken as a whole, this collection of writings merges religious and secular themes and references, expresses optimism and despair, yearning and distancing, detachment and closeness, love and death, and has us travel through stones and sparks, letters and spirits, smoke and smile, songs and cries, east and west, hidden and revealed.

1 Paris

The melody   15-17
The device   19-25
The revolt   27-28
Lena   29-30

The melody

The Rabbi had asked Ron to sing the next song. No, it was not possible. Ron was here to observe as a voyeur. And he observed: the 15 or 20 Hasidim seated at the table turned their heads toward him, waiting for Ron to comply. No. Ron did not feel he was worthy of this honor. He could feel in his flesh the pressure of his wallet in the back pocket of his pants. When Ron arrived in Budapest, he looked if he could attend the "third meal" celebrated by the Hasidim on *Shabbat*. He figured that by returning to his country of origin, he would have a more authentic vision of the post-war Hasidic life.

Ron was caught by surprise to learn that the Hasidim were still meeting in 1977. Yanosh, a student in the rabbinical school—non-Hasidic, and the only rabbinical school in Eastern Europe at the time—had agreed to help him as a guide. He showed Ron the way but he did not enter the building. Obviously, Yanosh did not approve of Hasidic way of life, however he sympathized with Ron's curiosity.

Ron did not have time to change; he had to keep his wallet in his pants, despite the Sabbath prohibition. He was the only foreigner in the small room of the synagogue. Here, the men were all well over 60. The ambience was not hostile. With the exception of the Rabbi, all were clean-shaven, and none wore the traditional garb of the Hasidim, to the point where Ron wanted to verify that they would sing Hasidic songs. "Of course," answered a man protectively, as if talking to a young novice.

Ron had waited for that moment. During his tour of Eastern Europe, he planned to stay only three days in Budapest; however he arranged that one of those days would be during a Sabbath. He wanted to witness the legendary enthusiasm that engulfs the Hasidim during the "third meal," just before nightfall. Maybe, through their songs, they yearned to prolong a little more this already nostalgic moment that would reoccur only after a weeklong wait.

The afternoon service preceded the famous "meal." Ron went to sit on one of the benches with the others. The service was rushed as routine, and the Rabbi, dressed in his black caftan delivered a sermon in Yiddish. He seemed tired of reciting his monologue. The Hasidim listened politely, waiting for the end. Once the service ended, all headed towards the long table of rustic wood at the entrance of the room. The Rabbi sat at the end of the table and Ron again found the man who had greeted him, and they were sitting side by side. The "meal" consisted mainly of bread and marinated herrings.

And the Hasidim started to sing.

Ron had never heard anything like this. Rolling heads recited an unknown melody. The musical notes were there, and so were the words. The herring was here, and the table, and the synagogue, and the shaven Hasidim and the tired Rabbi. However, the original melody had disappeared here too, even in the old country.

Ron saw ghosts, survivors, elderly men repeating ancient rituals, already fossilized. The Rabbi, who must have noticed that Ron was following the words, reached out to him for the first time and asked him to sing. The wallet was almost burning in Ron's pants, but he could not refuse.

Ron recited the first stanza alone. The neighbor who had taken him under his wing moved aside a little. He whispered to Ron in the confident tone of an insider while elbowing him with a surprise mixed with respect: "But, this is Hasidic!"

Ron was surprised to hear some of the Hasidim singing the second stanza with him while trying to learn the melody, obviously new to them. Then the entire community joined in. The Hasidim seemed to be waking up from a long lethargy. Some even started to smile shyly, as if they just realized that they were not alone anymore in the world, as if in the new country where they had never visited, there were young people able to pass the flame.

Ron had come from Paris in search of an ancient melody and he found himself in a position of messenger, delivering a piece of life to music without soul.

May 25, 1992
New Haven, CT
Original French on pages 151-153

When he got up from the ground, a small ringtone like an electrical clock pierced the night, on the black sidewalk shining after the rain. A woman stood in front of the door at the edge of the sidewalk, next to the road. Maxim thought she was waiting for him and was even about to talk to him when the phone started to ring. "Hello? Could you…?" And the boss explained what had just happened and noted that according to him, the client would show up soon. Maxim had no time to be angry about having been interrupted from the meeting with his visitor, because at that moment he had almost forgotten her. However, Maxim had the feeling that something had happened and he was trying to recall the last instants before the phone call. The first image that returned to his mind was this shiny sidewalk after the rain, with the city

THE DEVICE

As usual, the salesman was in the store (a kind of perfume shop or something of the sort) when the telephone started to ring. "Hello? Have you got a…?" The customer began describing to him a rather complicated device which might have the consistency of plastic in an elongated spiral shape, somewhat like a small snail, but not exactly. "I am sorry, but you must be mistaken. We don't carry that." "Well, could you tell me the address of the shop?" The salesman gave it to him after a moment of surprise, meaning no harm nor giving a moment of thought as to how a customer could possibly know the telephone number without knowing the address. But once he had hung up, he suddenly experienced remorse and, not quite understanding why, he felt that he had just done

lights; and then the silhouette of someone dressed in dark clothing who was maybe about to talk to him. Maxim did not remember the shape of her clothes or their length. However, even if they were somewhat short, they most likely would have been covered by a coat or a raincoat of a more reasonable length. Maxim could not remember the words she may have uttered. In any case, he did not have time to dwell on this nonsense, since he had to get dressed quickly in order to go to the store. He was already too late and he would have time to think about this in the subway. He was now afraid of waiting too long, as his memory could fade away and he might even forget to remember what just happened. Especially, Maxim did not want the boss to call him to order again. In five years of service, this mishap happened to him only once. He put on his overcoat without taking the time to swallow his coffee. He had already confronted mostly sleepy and barely refreshed faces that appeared to be just out of their pillows, daubed with heavy makeup. Questionable smells merged with strong perfumes and scented lipsticks of passengers going to work. The short subway ride (too short, especially today) did not leave Maxim enough time to remember his visitor. What was so particularly important about what had happened? He thought that they had engaged in conversation. He stared discretely at the cute faces piled up around him, and he found himself trying to recognize his visitor among them. However, a passenger exhibited a contained impatience toward his little inspection, so he pulled up his newspaper to put on a good face for her. His eyes were grasping the big headlines something wrong towards his boss. He therefore dialed his boss's number and explained what had just occurred, indicating that in his opinion, the customer would not take long to show up. The boss abruptly came into the store a few minutes later. Without taking the time to remove his overcoat, he hurried towards the shop window and removed an ordinary box of soap which was prominently displayed, a sort of oval or rectangular plastic box of a soft pink or light blue color. Paying no attention to his employees, the boss opened up the little box and took out the "device." The problem now was to hide the empty box, for it might appear suspicious and give some indication which could lead all the way to the... "device." Wasting no time, the boss went into the back of the boutique. There were some black cardboard boxes of various sizes lying around, containing bulk quantities of perfume, possibly with of the first page folded in four, but his mind enjoyed imagining his meeting with his visitor. "Are you looking for someone?" had she asked him? Maxim remembered that he had not been surprised by this question asked so naturally. As a response, he must have uttered some clichés, which did not really satisfy him. However, it might have been he who had asked the question. Maxim was annoyed to be pulled out of his daydream in order to get off at his subway stop. That was the moment he realized that he had forgotten the plastic soapbox. He had not paid too much attention to the boss's request on the phone, and at the time, his thoughts were not really clear. And then, while rushing to get dressed, he had tried to recall his interrupted meeting and had performed only automatic gestures. Without really realizing why, he felt some remorse and sensed that he had caused problems for his boss. Maxim was already close to the shop and could see the storefront. He could barely discern a surprised look from the other employees when he greeted them. This reassured him a little. The salesman took his regular place while trying not to show any emotion, and he set up the display window, as was usual at this time of the day. It seemed that something was missing from the window. The salesman searched for which object it might be when the phone started to ring. "Hello? Do you have a...?" and the client started to describe to him a rather complicated device, which could have had the consistency of plastic, with a long spiral shape. "I am not certain that we still have it in stock, as it is rather an old model, but we could order it." This was again one of those routine phone calls bars of soap and other cosmetics, such as lipstick. But, in any event, there were certainly bottles of perfume of different size or number depending on the dimensions of the cardboard cases. The boss picked out the biggest case and cleanly tore off the top, going around the edges. Then, he took out the largest bottle of perfume and perhaps several other small items. When the bottom of the large cardboard box had been cleared out, he placed the empty little box inside, then put back in order first the small items, then the large bottle, and closed down the cardboard cover. At this very instant, the customer entered the shop. Perhaps he again asked for the device but, assuming hypothetically that he did so, the boss would surely have pointed out that this was a perfume shop and that they didn't sell that in perfume shops. In any case, it is certain that the customer did ask for perfume. The qualified salesman displayed familiar to the salesman; however this time Maxim had a déjà vu experience. Maybe he had heard this voice before. He took advantage of a delivery to bring along with him a young saleswoman in training, under the ironic but discreet smile of the cashier. Maxim rang the bell at the address of the client while looking at the camera above the door. It opened electronically and Maxim introduced the young saleswoman. They entered a vestibule ending in two doors. Above was written in big letters: SECURITY. On the left was inscribed the word: WOMEN; and on the other: MEN. The saleswoman turned toward Maxim to check if there was some danger, but he explained that it was better to comply with the security rules. After entering a small hall, Maxim faced a receptionist seated behind a glass counter. She was charged with taking the newcomer's clothing and personal effects and arranging them on a hanger. In exchange the visitor was supposed to receive a numbered bracelet, made of red plastic, as well as the complete rules and regulations of the house. When Maxim complied, the female receptionist operated an electronic door and he entered what he understood to be a waiting room or an observation lounge. The room, of medium size, rectangular, was lacking all furniture except for a modern bench consisting of a small metal beam supporting five or six seats without feet, spaced one from each other; the kind of bench found in a waiting room of a hospital. However, curiously, there were no lower tables where usually a few magazines are displayed for the patients. Maxim chose to sit on the seat next to the one on the end while avoiding the middle seats. Although there was no window or mirror their various products, emphasizing the advantage of buying whole cases. The customer requested a case of the largest size containers. The qualified salesman went into the back of the store, his boss observing him with a satisfied look. The salesman searched around for the cases of large size containers, but there remained only one. He came out and presented it to the customer intending to wrap it up in the usual fashion. At this moment, the boss noticed that there was a tear on the cover of the cardboard box. He snatched away the package and under some pretext, dashed into the back of the shop, passing in front of the cashier whose sarcastic yet discrete smile demonstrated that he clearly knew all along what he was up to. The boss opened the cover of the big black cardboard box, took out the large bottle of perfume, and removed the empty little box. Afterwards, he slid the perfume bottle into the (which could have been used for one-way observation), Maxim figured that he was being observed, and while attempting to act naturally, he tried to show himself in the most positive light. He was somewhat disturbed by his lack of clothing, although much less so than if he had not been alone in the room. There was no noticeable smell in the room and it was brightly lit from the ceiling, probably by fluorescent lights. There was no audible noise, even from streets nearby. Maxim did not have his watch anymore, as it was taken at the entrance, and no clock hung on the walls. In order to count time, Maxim had the idea of taking his pulse. However the method was not reliable, since his pulse could vary during the day. Maxim knew that well, as he had consulted a physician for this kind of

22

problem, which had been resolved. Although he did not notice it when he entered the room, Maxim now felt it to be a little hot, albeit not to the point of sweating. He thought it would be wise to remain seated; an attempt to open one of the two doors would probably be misinterpreted and could backfire. In any case, it was most likely that those doors could be operated only from the outside and probably electronically, like the front door. Progressively, Maxim found that his mind became garbled, that his head was heavy, and that his heart was beating faster. He tried to check his pulse as his doctor had taught him, but his movements were imprecise and he had difficulty finding the right spot. Maxim couldn't concentrate his diffuse thoughts and he was making mistakes while counting the pulsations. When he stopped, he could not remember at all the previous number. Maxim was now sweating profusely. He started to feel dizzy and he was so weak that, despite his effort of staying nicely on his seat, he slipped slowly and found himself lying on the floor next to the bench. Maxim was still holding in his fist the wrinkled sheet listing the house rules, but he was not aware of it anymore. A few images rushed into his head and then faded away beyond his control. Maxim glimpsed a memory of the ironic but discreet smile of the female cashier when he had left the store, the impatient look of the subway passenger, the moment when he went down the street with his visitor and when he thought of his response which had not really satisfied him. Maxim was seeing again in his mind the young saleswoman he had brought along with him; and, trying to regain control of his thoughts, he wondered

narrow space provided for it inside the cardboard box. He then closed the top and returned the package to the customer, who departed. The boss then felt like explaining everything to his employees, but already, like children, they were creating a ruckus, and two of them were even leaving the store hand in hand as if nothing unusual were going on. They were already at some distance when the boss had to step out of the store and call out to them at the top of his lungs. But they totally ignored him. "If you don't return right this instant, you're fired!" The boss's shouting seemed to have the desired effect, since they did come back, but with a touch of arrogance toward the boss, who felt that he had gotten the worse of this affair. But, as he had decided to explain himself to his employees, and they were romping around all over the shop, he announced: "Everyone to the meeting on the 6th floor." (Perhaps it was what could have happened to her. It was he who had encouraged her to enter the building and she had followed him. Still in a fog, Maxim believed that a doctor was examining him. He heard brouhaha of words and understood that they had searched his belongings and did not find any identification. He heard the young saleswoman saying that they had come for a delivery. Maxim heard vaguely some deliberations about him. Not knowing his religion, someone had decided to call a priest and a rabbi. The two clergymen consulted each other and decided that when in doubt, one would not give Maxim the Sacrament of Extreme Unction and the other wouldn't recite the kaddish. Maxim made a great effort to concentrate and prevent his ideas from flying away one after the other. He used the last of his energy to hang onto the first image that

the 7th or the 8th but certainly not the 5th.) He had intentionally assumed a matter-of-fact tone of voice as if it were no more than one of those routine meetings where everyone sits around quietly in his chair. But the employees were having a lot of fun. Playing tag or hide-and-seek and running around wildly, they rushed into the only elevator without waiting for the boss. A few of them may have taken the emergency stairway, unless it was just those who had already gone up by elevator who continued playing around in the stairway. In any case, the boss found himself alone in the shop, and when he got to the elevator, a little ringing sound like that of an electric alarm clock pierced through the laughter and noise of the employees running up and down the emergency staircase. The boss looked up toward the row of illuminated numbers

came to mind, that of the receptionist. When he was in the hall, Maxim did not think that he looked at the hostess precisely; however, images returned to his memory with an astonishing degree of accuracy. The hostess was seated at a narrow, almost square desk behind a glass cage. One could see the legs of the desk through the glass; black metallic tubes, slightly conical. At ground level, a layer of black rubber matting covered the of each leg The hostess sat on a round swivel chair covered in black leather (or possibly imitation leather) with a small lumbar support of the same materiel at her lower back, forcing her to curve it in order to sit up straight. Outside, the noise seemed to have diminished. The doctor was probably gone by now. Maxim heard the priest and the rabbi deliberating and, thinking that Maxim had by now finished his journey in this world, they also decided to leave. The room was getting empty and Maxim was probably alone when he remembered the familiar voice on the phone and, in a supreme effort, he articulated words he did not always know and which he surprised himself to pronounce:

...ENTICE

... MISPRICE...

VICE...

SPICE...

VICE...

DEVICE

above the door to see at which floor the elevator was on. But, instead of numbers, there appeared a flashing sign: **DANGER** (perhaps, in reality it said: "warning, danger") **BREAKDOWN** (perhaps this word did not actually appear, but it was quite possible): **A MALFUNCTION HAS OCCURRED** (or some similar phrase). This was not very clear. Who had caused this? One could assume that it was the employees who, while playing around, was at fault. As a result, the boss no longer felt like explaining anything to his employees. But above all, he was afraid that they would hang around the store running all over the place, for he knew that he could not make them get out. He was quite relieved to see that the employees exhibited no desire whatsoever to remain on the premises, but rather preferred to horse around outside as the first two had done before he called them back. When all the employees had gone out, the boss likewise went out and closed down the floor lock at the bottom of the glass door.

Paris, 1978 - 1985

Text in bold: Translation by Adrian P Gonzalez M, adapted by the author
Original French on pages 155-162

Device (Urban Dictionary)
1: A line of sh*t told to gullible dumb asses. "He'll spend a lot of time controlling the border. He may not spend very much time trying to get Mexico to pay for it. But it was a great campaign device." -- Newt Gingrich. By Expat Chronicles 11/16/2016
2: An object that is required to complete the task at hand, e.g. TV remote, mobile phone, condom, spliff. Elenor: I need a device Alexis: Coming up honey... By TBV 4/16/2008
3: A very hot woman. Look at that hot device! Check out that device! By deerga_sid 6/17/2005 & by D.P.Lipsky 3/17/2004
4: A nerdy word for a tool. That kid Mack is a device! By deerga_sid 6/17/2005
5: The primary male genital organ aka penis aka cock, sometimes it is mechanical-like in nature. Bob has a very small device. Too big a device is a real thing. By Meeja 6/19/2017
https://www.urbandictionary.com/define.php?term=device (accessed 12/31/17)

The revolt

It was lunchtime at the canteen of a primary school. Maurice would never have remembered the canteen and its joyful meals if not for a serious incident, which had disturbed the carefree small child he was then.

Maurice did not remember what they were eating or if he was hungry—he probably was—nor how old he could have been. He could only remember that he was in the early classes of the primary school and that he was seated by chance, or rather because of the supervisor, at a "big kids" table. Obviously, judging from each dish, the "big kids" always took the largest portions and left the smallest for Maurice. It was mean, but he could not say anything. It was normal.

Maurice remembered now that it was spring. The sun was shining. The sparrows were whistling happily in the courtyard trees. His back faced the sun, which diffused softly its dusty light into the large dining hall. A large fly fluttered here and there through laughter and chatter. Maurice followed the fly and found her fun to watch. Next to him, the big kids were laughing hysterically, doubled over by a joke one of them had made. The fly looked very happy to see them all excited this way. She was moving very slowly in order to observe each child longer. And here she was above them, next to the table.

Suddenly, one of the "big kids" raised an empty glass and trapped the fat fly against the table. He screamed triumphantly: "Hey, she has the right to die!" Maurice lost his temper and replied pathetically, "She also has the right to live!" Then, helpless, he witnessed the fly's agony. The big kids cut her wings and her legs and finally they smashed her. A chill went down Maurice's spine. The big kids frightened him. He moved back. He saw them laugh, proud of their bravura.

Maurice suddenly had the urge always to remain little. It was absurd, of course; however he did not want to reach the big kids' saddening age. He saw again the crushed fly, the madness of the big kids, their foolishness. Maybe men were bad? Therefore he was bad. No, he was not bad; he was a child, not a man. He would become bad. He was disoriented, terrified by the future. He did not want to become like the big kids. Never. But what could he do?

Paris, December 14, 1971
Original French on pages 163-164

Lena

Her friends, who came from everywhere, accompanied her from Boston to the *shmate* district in Paris on a gray and cold winter afternoon. They gathered in the alley in small groups, sorted by family and acquaintanceship. They would have been happy to meet outside here on another occasion.

"Be careful" said a rather tall man with a strong and firm voice, who appeared to be in charge of the ceremony. "For RoTenberg, it is that way, for RoZenberg it is here," he enunciated, accentuating the different consonants. The relatives followed the dark car to her last journey, till the alley of the peupleraies-peoplecrying. With precise gestures, the man pulled out two folding stools, which he placed in front of the crowd, apart from each other at a calculated distance. Then with the same impersonal and professional tone, he asked for volunteers to transport Lena on top of the stools. A faded red-orange flag, its used velvet cloth discreetly torn downward and stiffened on the left by a mast as seen in a veterans' march, was laid flat. On the flag was written simply, in French only, a unique concession to the language of Lena's adopted country: *Cercle Amical* (circle of friends), a watered down translation from the original Yiddish *Arbeiter Ring*, the Workers' Circle.

We could have taken him for a Rabbi, with his red beard and his grayish checked cap. He spoke about Lena in Yiddish only; a clear Yiddish that even the Sephardi Jews could understand. He spoke of the little Lena, of Lena the woman, the mother, the polyglot intellectual.

A detail of the organization must have slipped away from the vigilance of Szulem, her husband: Probably out of a routine respect for Jewish customs, the bareheaded master of ceremonies invited only males to carry Lena. Why? Lena, the free thinker, challenging traditions, a feminist before her time, wouldn't she had been proud to be carried to her resting place by at least one woman?

New York, February 24, 2005
Original French on page 165-166

2 New in America

New in town   33-34
In a cloud of smoke   35-38
Let's go, children   39-41
The last leaf   42-43
Words' cemetery   45
A pink short coat   47-48
We will be back   49-50

New in town

I have lived in New York for a few years and I have discovered some bizarre professions, such as dog walker and baby-proofer. In case you didn't know, a dog walker collects many dogs from their busy and wealthy owners and walks them in the streets. There is also a dog gym for the dogs to be able to smell each other in an enclosed space, when they aren't out strolling with their dog walker. A baby-proofer is a grownup who spends his time on all fours, sees the world from the point of view of a wild toddler, and thinks about each exciting place into which a child can introduce fingers, such as an outlet or stuck in the door of the parents' closet. For this he is highly paid, corresponding to his level of education.

When I was new in town, still a student recently arrived from Paris, I found out about a profession unheard of to me. I had a limited budget no letter of recommendation or paystub. Therefore, I looked at the classified ads of a Hasidic newspaper in Yiddish for someone ready to sublet a cheap studio. The apartment I found was in the Williamsburg section of Brooklyn, only a five-dollar cab ride from Greenwich Village. The neighborhood was poor and inexpensive but safe, an unusual combination at that time in the city. In the neighborhood resided Hasidic Jews from Hungary, pretty much all of them survivors of the Holocaust, or their descendants.

In New York, around 1990, we needed to be careful about security; and this area was like an island of security in the midst of questionable neighborhoods. I lived in a building without an elevator, a little rundown, no doorman. I did not have many friends who knew of my apartment, and I didn't expect anybody to show up unannounced. This is why I was surprised when one day the bell rang without warning.

First, I thought about security. I looked through the peephole and discovered a man dressed in a blue uniform, perhaps working clothes, who was waiting patiently. I opened the door and noticed that he was carrying a metallic object, a device with a long and thin neck. "I am the exterminator," he said. I didn't understand the word. However—and despite the polite attitude of this exterminator, who did not behave like a usual angel of death—I figured he had something to do with the extermination of Jews during the Holocaust that almost annihilated my ancestors and the ancestors of the neighborhood residents. That word had other associations for me, too: it was still possible to see advertising in the streets for *The Terminator* (the first movie), showing Arnold Schwarzenegger with his naked and muscular shoulders holding an oversized machine gun. I also thought of an older movie by Luis Buñuel, *The Exterminating Angel*. In any case, those associations were not very reassuring, and I closed the door rapidly, mumbling, "Thank you, we don't need it."

Now I don't laugh about those jobs and their funny names. On the contrary, I beg for the exterminator to come sooner and eradicate my cockroaches; and I also paid a lot for the advice of a baby-proofer. And if I had a dog, who knows what kind of help I would be prepared to seek?

New York, September 11, 2005
Original Hebrew on pages 167-168

In a cloud of smoke

The small flowers were cut out of cloth. Some were white as the blossoms on a bridal bouquet, others with green leaves. The woman in a raincoat walked up and down the ranks of men and each of them picked a flower, red or white. They either held them between their fingers or stuck them in their lapels.

Kalman was watching the scene with detachment, as though what was happening could not possibly affect him, as though the whole thing were a show that had little to do with him.

It was chilly. The sky was grey and Kalman had been wise to bring along a scarf to protect himself from the wind.

"Gather ranks," the Master of Ceremonies commanded the members of the chorus, and he extended his arms to draw them together. Kalman felt a mixture of surprise and unease. To justify his compliance in his own eyes, he told himself that he would be warmer this way. Then he smiled to himself and continued to play the game. For a fleeting moment, he had an absurd vision of himself elbow to elbow with strangers on a lonely patch of grass stuck between a noisy highway and a muddy bank. The woman who was handing out the flowers left the group of mourners and walked toward the chorus. Once again, Kalman had a brief moment of unease when he realized that he, too, had to pick a flower. He had to choose the color quickly. He decided to pick the nearest flower. A moment later, Kalman realized that the red flower was prettier and more genuine, but it was already too late, so he stuck the stem in his buttonhole.

Kalman had felt the same discomfort when he had attended a performance of Handel's *Messiah* for the first time and, to his surprise, the crowd rose for the last movement. Kalman had gone along with them, telling himself that he would see better that way. The second time, he stood up with everyone else. He felt no further need to justify his action; only felt self-conscious to honor a religion that had persecuted his ancestors.

The Master of Ceremonies said a few words in front of the V-shaped, black marble monument. Kalman was watching the veterans who made up the group of mourners. Some were wearing their medals or decorations on their caps or their leather jackets. A woman and a young child were comforting a pony-tailed man in his 40s. Then, the instruction was given to lay the flowers on the foot of the monument; everyone at his own pace. Without a moment of hesitation, the man with the pony tail led the way.

Kalman waited his turn; he was careful to go neither too early nor too late. Like the others, he walked up to the monument, bent down, and slipped his flower into the crown of twigs that resembled the crown of thorns worn by Christ in his passion. Then he went back to his place and closed ranks once again.

Contrary to what he had supposed, Kalman was not able to keep his flower. Now he wasn't sorry he hadn't picked the red flower, and his initial concern seemed absurd. A few weeks later, Kalman by chance noticed a basket filled with candies wrapped in green netting. After asking permission to take one, he untied the stem of the red cloth flower that held the small package shut. He read the label: "Made by handicapped Vietnam Veterans," and he threw away the red flower, without noticing it was the same kind that he had been attracted to before.

The ceremony went on, and no one in the assembly seemed quite sure of his role. The Master of Ceremonies directed the chorus of voices belonging to the staff as they responded in unison to the group of Veterans: "We give you permission to free yourself from the spirits of the dead who have been haunting you since the war. Let those spirits rejoin the natural elements, the earth, the sky, the sea, and let yourself find inner peace."

One at a time, the Veterans stepped up to a large metal urn and read aloud the names of the spirits who haunted them, and the staff repeated their words. Some Veterans did not recite a single name, and some listed many. One said simply, "the men on the bridge." What had happened on the bridge? One could guess only too well. Each man dropped into the urn a slip of paper inscribed with the names, like the Hasidim who insert their prayers into the Wailing Wall.

Then the Master of Ceremonies lit the papers in the urn and Kalman saw, in the space of an instant, the spirits burned alive detaching themselves from the letters of their names and floating up to the gray sky in a cloud of smoke, just as the smoke from the ovens of Auschwitz must have drifted toward the sky. Kalman was angry at the Master of Ceremonies for having invented that part of the ritual, but his anger dissipated when he saw the emotions of the Vets.

Finally, the ashes were scattered over the sea, as in a cremation rite. Nonetheless, Kalman couldn't prevent himself from thinking about Eichmann's trial. His ashes, too, had been scattered over the sea.

It was almost time for the end of the ceremony: a flower bulb was planted over the remaining ashes. The two groups of veterans and other staff were dissolved, and everyone held hands in a circle around the flower pot for a moment of silence.

So, Kalman had participated in the burial of other men's ghosts. Maybe it was time for him to bury his own.

January 22, 1992
New Haven, CT
Translation by Renée Passy Alfandary, adapted by the author
Original French on pages 169-172

Let's go, children

Allons enfants de la patri-i-e...[7]

The song surrounded Ben Gross, albeit with calm, as if it were a prayer. The lyrics were also new, far from this hymn, much too warlike in Gross' eyes. And Gross did not really have any patriotic fervor for his country of origin, which had permitted the *Vel' d'Hiv* roundup[8].

Softly, like a murmur coming from the four corner of the big room, paced by the Master of Ceremonies' fist on the podium, the regulars sang with seriousness and without much enthusiasm.

The group of visitors looked at each other at the beginning of the song. Gross had been a foreigner for quite some time, and he had lost the habit of socializing with his fellow countrymen. Just by looking at them, Gross felt he knew them better than the locals. He observed them with pleasure. He was curious about their dress code: only one had fully adopted the local attire, while others wore a costume or a jacket; one looked at ease in his sweatshirt, which praised, in French, Operation Desert Storm; another, with his three-day beard and a black T-shirt under his jacket, would have blended in totally at a nightclub on Saturday night. Gross imagined him choosing this black T-shirt which, while fashionable, would also fit in with the somber outfit of the regulars.

---

[7] Let's go, children of the fatherland (French national anthem).
[8] *Vel' d'Hiv:* The Winter Stadium. See:
http://www.yadvashem.org/yv/en/holocaust/france/vel_dhiv_roundup.asp

The visitors were simple people, most of them businessmen, who reminded him more of the Mellah[9] than of the heartland of France; Gross thought that, back in Paris, he did not used to identify with them.

After a moment of hesitation, the visitors, who were discreet during the entire service, picked up the song proudly and gave it a nationalistic energy, as if this song legitimized completely their presence in the community. The regulars seemed to lower their voices in the face of this unexpected enthusiasm.

Gross was also a visitor. He had chosen to mingle with this group that he had not expected to meet. He did not know that about 60 people came from Paris especially for this weekend; however, after cruising in the big room of the synagogue, which contained easily two or three thousand people, Gross ended up noticing them. In addition, the group had stormed the small podium behind the emcee, where they had a commanding view of the entire room.

Allons enfants… Gross started to sing with an amused enthusiasm, as if he too was part of the group. He had needed—and Gross figured that it was probably the same for the other visitors—to come to Brooklyn at the grand court of the *Lubavitcher Rebbe,* in order to reconcile himself, for just a moment, with his national anthem. He had decided to spend a Shabbat in Crown Heights with a few friends from Manhattan, and he had found France, and a Paris he thought he had forgotten.[10]

---

[9] Mellah: Popular Jewish quarter in North Africa.
[10] This Lubavitch tradition of singing the French national anthem with Hasidic words was started in 1973 by the last Lubavitcher Rabbi, in order to hasten the coming of the messiah. Already, and for the same purpose, the first Lubavitcher Rabbi converted a march from the Napoleon imperial army into a Hasidic song. See the video of this song:

May 10, 1992
New Haven, CT
Original French on pages 173-175

http://www.chabad.org/therebbe/livingtorah/player_cdo/aid/297181/jewish/Hoaderes-Vhoemunah.htm

The last leaf

The last leaf of the tree
Has fallen
The last color of the street
Yellow, red
And six months of my life

The last leaf of the tree
Will fall
Its yellow will brighten the street
And my life

The last day of my life
Has slipped
The last heat
The last gaze
The last color

The last day of the life
Will fall
Its gaze will brighten the street
And my tree

December 6, 1990
New Haven, CT
Original French on pages 177
Drawing by the author

Words' cemetery

Pointed
Slanted
Twisted

Kettle
Pebble
Doodle

Pou
Ouag
Dg

Tear^{oom}
The Rajfra discuss philos.
L'ébouillanthé

Master KeyWord

Invent new words
Which would mean nothing
To you
Forget the old words
Bury them

In the cemetery of words

March 16, 1991
New Haven, CT
Original French on pages 179

A pink short coat

First the curiosity
It couldn't work
A shame to make her waste time
Dried flowers in rosewater
In the stationary
But not the usual tale of the
"Down to earth" and the
"With a sense of humor"
Young "working in Jewish Studies"
But this answering machine
This high pitch voice decisive
Forceful professional impersonal

A brunch
Which shouldn't last
Which wasn't meant to last
Earrings
Short blond curly hair
Spiral earrings
A necklace tight around the neck
Knotted strictly
A brunch that could not last

A brunch
A stroll through the Village
In the cold
A café
A billiard game, a real billiard
Take the tickets for the evening
A café with too much light
Helping two handicapped in a wheelchair
To go down from the sidewalk
Objectively nice but rational

A jazz club
The first session
A light in her eyes
When she thought I was educated
The sight of her naked neck
When her scarf came undone
The scarf tied again, conscientiously

The second session
Her way of accepting a hand
Of waiting and slowly imitating
Her hand sometimes humid
Her way of letting herself be kissed on the neck
Below the scarf

And then the taxi
The taxi driven by a woman
The taxi which passes her apartment
And has to make a detour
Blessed be the taxi

A strange idea
Tell the friends
To marry at the synagogue with a Rabbi
With a Rabbi
To marry with a Rabbi.
A child at school
Answering a question
"My father is a psychiatrist,
My mother is a Rabbi"

A Rabbi in a pink short coat

New York, February 21, 1990
Original French on pages 181-182

We will be back

"**1**; 25; 14; 30" The small journal listed the anniversaries
"50; 60; 88" and the birthdays.
"Romantic; Special place; Charming."
The Labor Day and Memorial Day weekends were the most popular.
"We will be back, promise." However, no new entry in the small book.

What became of them? All those couples who spent the night in the four-poster bed in front of the fireplace, looking to rejuvenate their relationships.

Were they still together or separated by death?
Were they still able to make love?
Was she withered by age and he by rheumatism?

The place looked redone. No TV. Only some "quality time" to spend with the spouse.

And the illegitimate couples? They did not leave a trace in the small book, marking their passage only by the absence of an entry during the most popular weekends.

"Eggs Benedict, quiche, delicious breakfast, caring hostess."
Who was reading the little book? Who thought of answering and did not?
Who was surprised to realize that this bedroom was not really theirs, not only for them?

Who answered to the small book?
The woman, with round and polished writing, as if in her diary.

Who apologized for being here?
Who did not feel they belonged to the club
And cruised embarrassed through the entries of the small book?

No, it was not possible.
Before discovering this collective diary
The place appeared to be ours,
Without ghost, without past,
Flowing in time

And love.
Make love.
Replay the wedding night
And the tenderness.

We will be back.

June 22, 1995
Original French on pages 183-184

3 Jerusalem

Missing Jerusalem   53-55
Days of Awe - High Holidays   57-61
In the center   63-64
Hitnatkut (A house destroyed)   65-66
Insha'Allah (God willing)   67-68
Israeli fashion   69

Missing Jerusalem

A piece of Jerusalem is missing, and I did not find it.
I found unexpected relics of Jerusalem
Like a long forgotten love letter in the yellowish pages of a book;
Melodies and people from a Sephardic Synagogue
I used to frequent on Friday nights in Paris.

I also found new pieces of Jerusalem:
Scent of colorful flowers and songs of birds at dawn;
Fresh mountain air in the evenings.
And incongruent pieces of Jerusalem:
Tall pine trees of my childhood forests in France;
Crows cutting up a dead cat in the street.
I found old and familiar pieces of Jerusalem:
The Western Wall of my Bar Mitzvah...
And around the corner, the "Kotel of the Birds,"
As my daughter Leah called the Southern Wall at sunset,
With their myriads of songs merging into the pink light and the stones.
There, I found new seeds of Jerusalem
Being planted in the burgeoning and amazing spirituality of Leah.

I have been looking for the missing piece of Jerusalem, but I did not find it.
I found fragments of Jerusalem belonging to others:
Cesare, a salient fellow Ulpan student
Exiting the Pontifical Biblical Institute, next to the French Consulate;
This Christian at the Kotel
Who came from Switzerland with others to pray in Jerusalem for Sukkot;

Amir, our Arab contractor
Who knew how to find giant old stones in the old city's
   Muslim quarter;
The Arab taxi driver who wished me "Hag Sameach"
When he drove me to the old city on Tisha b'Av,
After we exchanged prayers for peace and coexistence in this
   spiritually thick city.

I found pieces of the real economy of Jerusalem:
The used pair of shoes which, unlike in other years,
Some of Leah's playmates cannot afford to buy;
An industrial and commercial district of Jerusalem, Talpiot,
   bursting with activities;
Malls as big as in North Carolina where, here too, teenagers
   like to hang out;
The warning by both our daughters' teachers
To eat breakfast before school, as hunger prevents learning.

A piece of Jerusalem is missing, and I did not find it.
The joyful voice of our Rabbi singing *Sh'hekheyanu* on
   Simchat Torah
At length with wit and humor;
The familiar faces at the morning *minyan* at Or Zarua, where
   your presence really counts;
The warm family atmosphere at the Boro Park clinic where
   you feel you are doing holy work;
The teachings of Rabbi Wechsler to its Holy Congregation in
   front of the Eastern Wall.
These too are missing fragments of Jerusalem, yearning to be
   restored.

The following piece of Jerusalem was dictated by Leah, age 6, and has been inserted by Leah and her younger sister Miriam into a crack of the Western Wall:

"Dear Israel,
I hope you don't have any more wars,
I like being here a lot."

"Dear G-d,
I thank you for all that you have created.
The people that I love and the animals that I try to take care of.
Thank you for making me."

May the simple prayers of children like Leah's help fill up all the cracks of the Walls of Jerusalem and build the foundation of the restored Jerusalem.

Jerusalem, October 19, 2003

Days of Awe—High Holidays

Old Katamon, Jerusalem
11th of Tishrei, 5764; October 7, 2003

Dear Amira,

Happy New Year to you and all your family! We are getting organized slowly but surely. We don't yet have a living room sofa (the sofa we wanted to buy is apparently stuck in the port of Ashdod because of a strike), however we have a *sukkah* in our garden. You can see what are the priorities in Jerusalem! This is our first High Holiday in Israel, and I would like to share with you, as I explained to my friends in Paris and New York, what I experienced when I returned from *shul*.

On Friday night, which was also *Rosh Hashanah*, I did not wish "happy new year" to anyone on my way back from the synagogue. Not because there was nobody to greet; on the contrary! More than on a regular *Shabbat* eve, there were many families in the street leaving synagogues, unknown to me, but with pleasant faces as if they were familiar, like the dear faces of friends gathered at a Shabbat table. I heard Hebrew, English and French. I could have invited any of them to our festive table. In New York, and for sure in Paris, if someone were wearing a *kippah* or it was obvious that she was returning from shul, at least someone would have looked at us and wished us a happy new year. Here, nothing. I had the urge to imitate the naïve cowboy from the movie *Crocodile Dundee* who greeted everyone in the crowds of midtown Manhattan. Then I understood what is so special about being Jewish in Jerusalem: To be part of a majority, and not so special after all.

Don't worry, our neighborhood is very friendly, and we keep getting invitations for Shabbat and holidays. They meet us in shul or even at our doorstep, and greet us warmly. And people have been so helpful in the street. For example, when we asked where the post office was, someone drove us there without us asking, and despite being busy himself. And yes, people say *shalom* to us in the streets... sometimes. Many told us that they feel a responsibility to help new immigrants. They were enthusiastic to help us, as if it was necessary that we feel good in the beginning of our integration in Israel, maybe for the sake of the survival of Israel. Most had themselves been new immigrants in the past, and they told us that they also received help. It seems that they are happy to find an occasion to pay back what they received from others, and the message is clear: "We do not expect anything from you, we are just returning what we received already. Your responsibility is to return this, after a few years, to other new immigrants. Because of this, the country will continue to exist."

Yesterday, *Yom Kippur* was even at a higher level. First of all, during the preceding days, the radio interviewed soldiers, veterans of the Yom Kippur war, in memory of its 30th anniversary, and they asked them if a similar situation could repeat itself today. After that, the terrible terrorist attack hit the restaurant in Haifa. And then, on the Kol Israel radio station during the afternoon of Yom Kippur eve, we could hear only very brief news. The BBC explained in more detail the response attack by the Israeli army, which bombed a terror camp it Syria. Israeli national radio broadcasted only cantorial music of Yom Kippur—Sephardic and Ashkenazic, of course—and the new Israeli version of the *Unetaneh Tokef* prayer[11]: "Who will live, and who will die." And then, without any warning or even a news summary, exactly at 4 PM, one hour before candle lighting time, all the Israeli radio stations

---

[11] *Unetaneh Tokef*: An intense High Holiday prayer.

stopped after singing *Hatikvah*, the Israeli national anthem, and a final announcement about resuming broadcast the next day after Yom Kippur. Period. Deadly silence. Not even recorded music to remind us that the radio (or the country) still existed.

Days of Awe; Terrible Days!

I knew that on Yom Kippur, the country rested and was disconnected; however it is different to experience it. I remember when 30 years ago in Paris, Motele, the son of the Rav Chaim Yaakov Rottenberg, peeked over the shoulder of a less observant Jew who had joined our prayers in our synagogue on Yom Kippur, in order to read in the afternoon newspaper about the war just launched against Israel. Normally, Motele would never have even thought of profiting from a newspaper bought by a Jew on Yom Kippur, but it was a time of emergency. Maybe because of the information caught by his son, the Rav, a tall, impressive and charismatic rabbi with a long and neat white beard, usually restrained and not prompt to effusive displays of piety, decided unexpectedly to take the stand for *Neilah*, the final Yom Kippur prayer.

The Rav had famously kept his faith intact even during the Nazi persecutions[12]. Once, the Rav illustrated in passing with a personal story, a small intimate teaching about the law related to the interruption of the standing silent prayer (*amidah*) in case of a life threatening emergency. During the war, he had been in a cell with prisoners sentenced to death, and he thought that he would share their end. While reciting that silent prayer, a German soldier approached him and talked to him. The Rav explained that normally this would have been a case of life threatening emergency, because not

---

[12] See: download.yutorah.org/2015/1053/Rosh_Hashanah_To-Go_-_5776_Rabbi_Weiss.pdf

answering a German soldier could have been punishable by death. However, at the time he thought he was already on death row and had nothing to lose; therefore he chose to continue his prayer. The German soldier saw this standing man mumbling to himself and took him for a disturbed person. He left the Rav unhurt, not realizing that he was praying. Later on, the Rav realized that he was placed in that cell accidentally, and was not actually slated for death row.

On that first day of the Yom Kippur war, the Rav delivered the final prayer with intensity, almost crying but also as a strong and loud defender of the Jews, especially when asking "Our Father, Our King, annul the thoughts of our enemies." I have never heard again such an intense and moving prayer, and I believe that the State of Israel survived 30 years ago not only because of our brave soldiers, but also because of that prayer and the merits of this exceptional man of faith.

Now in Jerusalem, on the morning of Yom Kippur, there were obviously no printed Israeli newspapers, and I wanted to ask the secular-looking guard at the door of our synagogue if he had listened to the BBC. However, he appeared calm and unconcerned about the current situation. I clearly could not have asked the guard at the synagogue nearby, a mature man with a long beard and an open prayer book in front of him, dressed in the traditional white High Holliday robe called a kittle, a heavy gun precariously tucked into its flimsy white cotton belt.

Coming back and forth to the synagogue was completely different during this warm Yom Kippur. Many children were riding bicycles in the middle of the street. During the 15-minute walk to shul— we did it four times that day—we did not see even one moving car. We possibly heard a fire truck, but no ambulance (and therefore, no terrorist attack). We are not living in the very religious neighborhood of Mea Shearim, and the streets were completely open to circulation during Yom Kippur. There were simply no cars; only a festive atmosphere of serenity and peace. Yes, peace. What is there to do during this great day if not to go to the synagogue or to ride bicycles? There was coexistence and even a partial overlap between those two worlds: it was possible to see boys wearing a kippah using rollerblades or a kicking a scooter. Another time, I saw a Hasidic boy standing in the middle of the street, and he did not move when a secular boy rode his bike in his direction rapidly while ringing his bell. In any case, it did not appear to be much of a big confrontation.

I did not get out this morning; however Sasha told me that around the corner, they are selling now palm branches for the holiday of *Sukkot*. Really an amazing neighborhood!

Again, happy new year. Your friend,

Gad

New York, September 25, 2005
Adapted from the original Hebrew

In the center

New York
December 17, 2005

Dear Amira,

I usually do not write much to my friends. However, two months after our arrival in Israel during the High Holiday season, I started writing to everyone, to explain my experience. Why? If I had moved to Jackson, Mississippi, I don't think that I would have written as much. Jerusalem is different. There is a responsibility towards those who stayed outside Israel. Everyone is looking at you, really, it is not paranoia; and you are obligated to explain. So, I explained, again and again, even after the anger, when all the words had disappeared, like after the terrorist attack on the café Hillel. Just to say that you are alive. In the beginning, you may remember that I sent you a letter about the holidays of the months of Tishri, when I was filled with enthusiasm.

More than a year has passed now, since our return from Jerusalem. And this too, I feel the need to explain. Jerusalem is a special, holy city. However, even its holiness can be overwhelming. Sometimes, I crave being in a regular place, far away from the center, a place not so special all the time, even boring. Our Rabbi told me that once he rented an apartment in the old city, and its windows were facing the Western Wall. "It was too much. It was disturbing to simply wake up in the morning in my pajamas and open the window, because of the sanctity of the place." For Sasha, even living in Israel for an extended period of time was too much, because we took care of simple day-to-day things, such as going to the local grocery store or to the laundry, and would forget how this place is so special. Sasha felt that our stay there was, so to speak, taking away from the sanctity of Jerusalem.

For me, it was the opposite. I loved the contrast between the celestial and the earthly Jerusalem, with its smell, its flowers and its dead cats in the streets. I loved the earthiness of Jerusalem, and also its sanctity, and most of the time, its centrality.

When we returned to New York, I found that things had changed. For example, it is impossible to feel completely miserable on *Tisha b'Av* at the Western Wall in Jerusalem. On the contrary, the masses of Jews who flock to the Wall on that day are like the beginning of a renewed promise unveiled to the Jewish people. One cannot contain an inappropriate joy (mixed with guilt) during this day of mourning Jerusalem's destruction.

Not so outside of Jerusalem. This too is a piece of Jerusalem, and I had to return to New York to discover it. Jerusalem is not complete until we experience its absence.

With blessings,
Your friend,

Gad

December 17, 2005
Translated from the original Hebrew

Hitnatkut
(A house destroyed)

Daughter of Zion
Your temple, ruined
Your oil, spilled.
Our house, demolished
Our garden, uprooted.

Your fortifications, breached
Your residents, exiled.
Our wall, cracked
Our children, scattered.

Your alliance, overturned
Your wedding canopy, deserted.
Our marriage contract, neglected
Our tallit, ripped.
Your Torah, abandoned
Our *mezuzot*, defective.

In the cracks of your wall, Jerusalem
Children will not stuff petitions.
Your Holy of Holies, open to the four winds
Our field, full of weeds.
Your orchard, without flagrance
Our pomegranates, without seeds.
Your face, hidden
Our gaze, apart.

חֻרְבַּן הַבַּיִת

בַּת צִיּוֹן
מִקְדָּשֵׁךְ נֶהֱרַס, שַׁמְנֵךְ נִשְׁפַּךְ
בֵּיתֵנוּ הָשְׁמַד, גַּנֵּנוּ שֹׁרַשׁ.

חוֹמוֹתַיִךְ נֻפְּצוּ, תּוֹשָׁבַיִךְ גָּלוּ
כָּתְלֵנוּ נִסְדַּק, עוֹלָלֵינוּ נִפְרְדוּ.

בְּרִיתֵךְ הֻפְרָה, חֻפָּתֵךְ נְטוּשָׁה
כְּתֻבָּתֵנוּ נִזְנְחָה, טַלִּיתֵנוּ נִקְרְעָה
תּוֹרָתֵךְ נֶעֶזְבָה, מְזוּזוֹתֵינוּ נִפְגְּמוּ.

בְּסִדְקֵי כָתְלֵךְ, יְרוּשָׁלַיִם
יְלָדִים לֹא יִתְחֲבוּ פְּתָקִים.
קֹדֶשׁ קָדָשֵׁיךְ לְאַרְבַּע רוּחוֹת
גַּנֵּנוּ לַעֲשָׂבִים רָעִים.
פַּרְדֵּסֵךְ בְּלִי רֵיחַ נִיחוֹחַ
רִמּוֹנֵינוּ בְּלִי גַּרְעִינִים.
פָּנַיִךְ נִסְתָּרִים
מַבָּטֵינוּ מַחֲלִיקִים הַצִּדָּה.

אִם אֶשְׁכָּחֵךְ יְרוּשָׁלָיִם
תִּשְׁכַּח יְמִינִי
תִּדְבַּק לְשׁוֹנִי לְחִכִּי.

If I forget you, Jerusalem
My right hand be forgotten
My tongue, glued to my
   palate.

Forget me, Jerusalem
Leave my right hand.
Leave my tongue in my palate
Leave my children in my
   bosom.
Leave my sleep in my eyes
Leave me alone, Jerusalem

What do I care about
   Jerusalem
When my garden is desolated
And my house destroyed.

תִּשְׁכְּחִי אוֹתִי יְרוּשָׁלַיִם
תַּעַזְבִי אֶת יְמִינִי.
תַּעַזְבִי אֶת לְשׁוֹנִי בְּחִכִּי
תַּעַזְבִי אֶת יְלָדַי בְּחֵיקִי.
תַּעַזְבִי אֶת שְׁנָתִי בְּעֵינַי
תַּעַזְבִי אוֹתִי יְרוּשָׁלַיִם

מַה אִכְפַּת לִי מִירוּשָׁלַיִם
כְּשֶׁגַּנָּתִי שְׁמָמָה
וּבֵיתִי חָרְבָה.

New York, December 2005
Translated from the original Hebrew

Insh'Allah (God willing)

How could we leave Jerusalem?

We don't feel guilty about leaving New York or Paris. "You want to leave? Good for you! Enjoy!"

Jerusalem is something else. We feel a responsibility towards others for being here; a responsibility not only towards the residents of the country, but also those who transformed us into emissaries and partners of the Jerusalem Dream.

How do we separate from Jerusalem, the center of the Jewish world, towards whom our hearts and our synagogues are directed? Impossible. More than with New York or Paris, we return with a piece of Jerusalem.

What piece of Jerusalem will we bring back? For sure our boy, born in Israel, and also our daughters who now are speaking Hebrew, and of course our private Jerusalem with our shared memories.

Our private Jerusalem will merge with other pieces of Jerusalem we found in New York and that are still missing in Israel, like the Congregation Or Zarua, our Rabbi, and the team at the clinic in Boro Park where we do holy work.

We will remember, not only the celestial Jerusalem
But also the earthly one
The birds waking up and singing at 5 in the morning, like
   now
The flowers, the stars in the sky
The pink air in the evening and the dry heat in the middle of
   the day
Our lovely neighbors and the pushy drivers

Our dedicated teachers, Esti and Chagit,
Who contributed to a meaningful experience for our
    daughters
With their classmates from the lower school and the
    kindergarten
And our friends from Hebrew classes at the Ulpan
And my cousin Michel
And the cats in the streets
And the airport
And the plane

But we will return to you, Jerusalem
God willing, *insh'Allah, si Dieu veut*

New York, November 24, 2005
Original Hebrew on pages 185-186

Israeli fashion

The Cast:
A) a pair of shoes with very high heels
B) a very low-cut pair of jeans
C) a wide leather belt (attached to "B")
D) a small black lace string bikini panty (reaching well above "C")
E) a heavy handgun in its holster (attached to "C")

The Scene:
Emek Refaim, a trendy street in Jerusalem, around the spring 2004.

The Action (view from the back):
At each step "A" wobbles. When "A" hits the ground, the heavy weight of "E" lowers "C" for a brief instant, creating a waxing and waning gap between the waistbands of "B" and "D".

New York, March 18, 2009

4 Longing for Jerusalem

In the streets of Jerusalem 73
Trilogy 75
A new stone 77
I looked 79

In the streets of Jerusalem

On the last days of summer
A poem of mine
Is walking the streets of *Yerushalayim*
Hopping up and down
To the sound of your steps

On the last days off before teaching
A poem of love
Is clinging inside your pocket
Flowing gently
To the rhythm of your legs

It makes your heart go faster
And mine too
In the streets of Jerusalem
And abroad

When will its writer
Have a chance
To be as close to you
Walking your steps
As this poem
On the last days of summer

New York, September 12, 2017

Trilogy

I have not yet given up
Finding someone interested
In moving with me to Israel

I like you Manhattan
Even better than Paris
And I love Paris
I am a *Manhattanien* by choice

However I see myself moving again
To Jerusalem
For a final journey
To finish the trilogy of cities
I love deeply
Each in her own way

Don't be jealous Manhattan
I will still love you
As I still love Paris

But the time is coming
I feel it
And I would like to share that excitement
With you

New York, September 10, 2017

A new stone

If I could I would be
An ancient stone
Foundation of the Temple
The stone where you put
All your devotion
And your lips
While praying to build
A new Jewish home
A new Temple
A new foundation
A new stone
A new kiss
A new love

If only I could

New York, August 28, 2017

I looked

I looked I looked and I looked

While I was at Shir Chadash
You were at its annex on Emek Refaim
Across from Sushi Rehavia
When I went to Yakar
You were not there anymore
Because someone smiled at you

I looked

Here I am
Where the West ends
And my heart is in the East
Where a new light
Will shine over Zion

I am looking

Still hoping to hear
The sound of your hair
Playing Zumba
To touch
The shadow of your hand
To smell
The field filled with your laughter
To taste
A pomegranate with you on the New Year

I will look

Hopefully soon
At you

New York, August 28, 2017

5 New York

Stones   83
As before   85-86
Till the end   87
The sparks between us   89
Butterfly words   91
Opera   93
Beth   95-96
Beth II   97
Cholent   99
Sparks   101
Shhh...   103
Ice breaker   105
Singing Questions   107-109
Last smile   111
That smile again   113-114
The Mirabeau Bridge   115
Blushing dress   117
Fire   119
A rose and a fox   121
People and places   123
Third wish   125
After the *chag*   127
Share a poem   129
Contained fire   131-132
Mechitza   133
Without love   135
Avi   137

Stones

Each *rencontre* is like a stone
Heavy rocks carrying the weight
Of aborted relationships
Stillborn romances
After each rock the load deepens
Making it more difficult
To move on
Till the stones cover you
Entombed

Each *rencontre*
Is like a stone
A precious stone
Sparkling to the sun
Like a poem
Which gives you joy
To read over
Again and again
They have names
They have faces
They lodge in your pocket
Ready to be picked up
And admired
One last time

New York, September 23, 2017

As before

Last night I saw you again

Last night through the glass window
At Deli Casbah
I saw you getting into the restaurant
With your long hair
Your red and black scarf tied up warmly
Around your neck
The red goes so well with your light skin
And your freckles
I was not sure
Your face was blurred in the dark night
You smiled at me widely
It's me through the window
Don't you recognize me
Yes of course you came
As a surprise
You knew I was meeting my kids here
Tonight at 7

The happiness of seeing your exited face
Happy to see me
As if it was normal
As before
As if nothing had happened

But how could you
Buenos Aires and Argentina are far away
You could not have made it
Even if you had wanted
I looked closer
I saw my daughter

So excited to see me
I was bouncing from joy too
When I recognized her
With her lovely red and black scarf
I bought her last year
Which suits her so well
The same I gave you
Shortly after we met

The sharp pain
Of realizing that probably
I just had the last glimpse
Of you

The serene joy
Having finally written
A poem about you
It will remind me your smile
Mixed with the love
Of my daughter

New York, February 9, 2018

Till the end

Till the ends of the world, I will make you laugh
Till the last drop in the shower, I will sing with you
Till *Motzei Shabbat*[13], I will eat with you
Till the credits of the movie, I will hold your hand
Till the finish line, I will run with you
Till the epilogue of your breath, I will hug you
Till, I will you

New York, Aug 8, 2016

---

[13] *Motzei Shabbat:* The end of the Sabbath, on Saturday night.

The sparks between us

The sparks
Between us.
The little pinch in the heart
Wondering if the other one understands
The energy

The fresh air
The intense awareness of the details
The little corner of your mouth smiling
Your hair translucent under the low sun
Your slightly trembling nose
The yearning

The passion, the fight
The rest, the sigh
The comfort, the resolution
Tenderness

Working, praying
Health, illness
Death, after-death

And, at last, returning to their divine source
The sparks

New York, July 2015

Butterfly words

Ah, you like words
You like to play with them
Maybe we can bounce
Words between us
Nicely
Hopping
Like a volleyball
Hoping
That we will never use them
One day
As a punching ball

Words of comfort
Words of teasing
Words of romance
Words of mouth
Words of ears and nose
Words of legs
Butterfly words

Mots de tête
Mots d'esprit
מילים חזקות   Strong words
מילים מתוקות   *Des mots doux* [14]
מי לי ?   *Mi li?* [15]
Maybe you?

New York, September 19, 2017

---

[14] Sweet/tender words (words = *milim*)
[15] *Mi li?* = Who is for me?

Opera

Of course I sing
The shower is my opera
I am known as the "Baal Shower Tov"

One summer I sang at the Opera in Rome
In front of the main door to be precise

My voice reverberated between
The buildings and the *Fiat Unos*

The mechanic down the street was so impressed
That he let me use his bathroom
For free

New York, August 28, 2017

Beth

Like you I enjoy life and relationships
Gam zu le tova Even that is for the best is my motto
I am loyal and honest
And now more generous
I like cooking, hiking, biking
Guests are often found in my home
On holidays and *Shabbos*.

I used to think I was smart
Now I try not to be a smartass
I want to be caring about others
And about you
Am I generous? I try.

I have seen the *Rebbe* at 770
And wrote about it
I am fascinated with Hasidism
I have studied and sometimes taught
Some of the *Tanya*, the *Sfat Emet*, *Kedushat Levi*,
Likutey Moharan, *Esh Kodesh* and others.
I have met many Hasidim and work with them.
My grandfather, may he rest in peace, was born a Hosid in Hungary.
And his father was a Rabbi.
But I am not a Rabbi, nor a Hasid, Beth.
I treat them, and talk to them every day,
I understand them, I pray with them,
Sometimes study with them,
Dance with them, study them
But I am not one of them.

I want to be open and share your life
Start a home full of warmth and respect

But Hasid I am not, Beth, my love, I am not.

New York, July 16, 2017

Beth II

I have that pinch in the heart
Telling me maybe you are the one
With whom I can rebuild
A Beth on earth and above
Not a second home
לא בית שני‎[16]
But the original one
The one that was never built
The one that should have been
A house for you and me
A house for all Jews
בית בשביל המקום
המקום שלנו‎[17]

New York, July 17, 2017

---

[16] Not a second home [in Hebrew]
[17] A house [Bayt/בית in Hebrew] for The Place (the Omnipresent); Our place

Cholent

Compassionate
Considerate
Outgoing
Totally loyal
That's four ingredients

We don't need more to make a Cholent
It takes time, simmering during the whole night of exile
But then we could savor it during the *Shabbat* of our
    relationship
Slowly, slowly till the end of days
Together
Till *Havdalah* would separate us
Only to meet again
Apart from this ephemeral world

Do you want to try?
It is only four ingredients...

New York, July 11, 2017

Sparks

Sparks, my dear
They are called sparks
Those ephemeral whimsical elusive flickering sparks
They flow along your long dark hair
They niche on your uncovered knees atop a high stool
They are in our heart and in our hands
They are not called whatchamacallit, my dear
Remember them my love?
They are called sparks sparks

New York, July 11, 2017

Shhh...

Don't know what to say?
Shhh...
Don't say anything
Love doesn't need words
Just feel the breeze around your neck
The taste of your coffee
Just peek at him
And see how much pleasure he has
In his eyes
Just sitting next to you

New York, July 2, 2017

Ice breaker

I just sent you
An automated "ice breaker"
To make your heart melt
Over chocolate fudge ice cream.

New York, June 7, 2017

Singing questions

I like a kind thoughtful person
I also love learning new things
It is not easy talking about ourselves
So I wrote a few questions for you

Are you pretty?
Are you smart?
Are you witty and bright?

Are you for me or are you not?
Will you love me or will you not?

Will you walk with me
Eat with me
Mend my socks
Milk the cow?

Will you let me
Cook your meals
Clean your house
Hold a hammer
Make you laugh?
Give you a massage
Take care of you
Just be with you?

Will you make *Shabbat* with me
Go to *shul*, learn with me?
Will you love my kids
And me yours
Would you be mine?

Will you fight with me, starve with me?
Will you be for the next
25 years in my bed?
Will you love Israel and visit it?
Will you live there one day with me?

Are you charming?
Is it alarming how charming you feel?
Are you modest and pure
Polite and refined
Well-bred and mature?

Are you stunning
And entrancing
Do you feel like running
And dancing for joy?
Will you be loved
By a pretty wonderful boy?

Will I make you feel dizzy
Sunny fizzy and funny and fine?
Will I know your name
Cell phone number, email
Instagram and Facebook page?
Will I see your latest picture
And learn your real age?

Tell me more, tell me more
Tell me more about you.
What you like, what you do
What you would like to do

I want to know all about you
All that matters to you
About your joy, about your pain
About your loss, about your gain
I want to know all about you

New York, May 27, 2017

Thanks to: Leonard Bernstein and Stephen Sondheim ("I Feel Pretty" from West Side Story*); Sheldon Harnick ("Do You Love Me?" from* Fiddler on The Roof*); Warren Casey and Jim Jacobs ("Summer Lovin'" from* Grease*); and Oscar Hammerstein II ("Getting to Know You" from* The King and I*).*

Last smile

All the friends and family gathered today are a testimony to how Daniel touched so many lives. His gentle approach and not-so-subtle humor made many smile across the world. It is amazing how he was able to retain so many friends all over, so many patient souls who listened to his poems and jokes with polite enthusiasm. He has tried so hard to be a *mensch*, and not to be so centered on himself. And for this effort, even if it was unsuccessful, we miss him dearly. Daniel wouldn't want us to cry tonight. He would like you to listen to his eulogy with an amused face.
Let us all send Daniel our last smile.

New York, May 24, 2017

That smile again

I

Cutiepie
I am drawn to your smile
Each time you appear on my screen
Finally I succumbed
So here I am

Oh, yes, you enjoy making people smile
Well, I can tell you
Your smile is contagious
I think I am already sick from you

II

And here again
Your smile shows up
And here I am
Bound to it

I said: Never again
Will I text her
But here she is
Smiling
Live on the screen

Should I block her
And cut the pain?

I don't have that courage, Cutiepie

Please block me

Please block me
And end my misery

Please block me
Please block me
Veil your face

May I not see your smile
Ever again

New York, November 27, 2016

The Mirabeau Bridge

The Mirabeau Bridge is pretty narrow
Most important: Do not fear
Love will flow once more
In your heart

Le pont Mirabeau

L'pont Mirabeau est bien étroit
Le principal: N'aie pas peur
L'amour coulera encore une fois
Dans ton cœur

New York, May 20, 2017
English translation from the original French
Thanks to: Guillaume Apollinaire (Le pont Mirabeau), and
Rabbi Nachman of Bratslav (Gesher tzar meod/The World is a Narrow Bridge)

Blushing dress

In a women's clothing store
She tried a few dresses
And then another one
I blushed
But did not know it

She noticed
"You are blushing!"
We were embarrassed
Because of the blushing

I must have liked her in the dress
A little risqué

She did not take the blushing dress
Then, I well understood why

Now
Not really

New York, September 19, 2017

Fire

I know
The water in the ocean is between us
And so is the earth under the water
And the air floating above the water
I know

I don't know
I am still thinking about the fire
The fire

Gently, very gently
Will I stroke this fire
With a faint blow in its neck
With a flowing hand
In its flickering hair

New York, May 23, 2017

Une rose et un renard | A rose and a fox

Stéphanie,	Stéphanie,
Une rose et un renard	A rose and a fox
Une boîte et un mouton	A sheep and a box
Un chapeau et un éléphant	A hat and an elephant
Stéphanie aussi...	And also Stéphanie…
Un petit prince endormi	A little prince asleep
Un ivrogne philosophe	A drunken philosopher
Un géomètre calculateur	A calculating geometer
Un allumeur réverbérant	A reverberating lamplighter
Stéphanie aussi	And also Stéphanie
On n'apprend qu'avec le cœur	We learn only with the heart
On n'apprivoise qu'avec le temps	We connect only with time
On ne drague qu'avec les mots	We seduce only with words
Veux-tu être mon amie?	Would you like to be my friend?

New York, October 26, 2016
English translation from the original French
*Homage to Antoine de St Exupéry (*Le Petit Prince, 1943*)*
*and to Fernandel (*Félicie Aussi, 1939*)*

People and places

People more than places

Paris
The light *la Seine*
So many memories
My first love
The place that used to be mine in *shul*
Now it belongs to a stranger
Who tried to be nice to me
When I visited

New York
My marriage
The birth of my girls
The Bobst Library at NYU

Jerusalem
The garden
Where my now 13-year-old son
Had his *brit milah*
The light making the Kotel pink
The Kotel of my Bar Mitzvah
And of my two girls
The birds singing at sunrise
The cats

People fused with places
People more than places

New York, July 19, 2017

Third wish

I would rather whisper my last wish in your ear
And ask you
What make your eyes shine
And how is the sun playing with your hair
If your fingers crush each other when you speak
If I could be privileged to hear your laugh
And if I can join the sun in its play

New York, June 9, 2017

After the *chag*

I will thank you
For stopping by
The Sephardic *kiddush*
To see me
Chag sameach! [18]

During the *chag*
I will think of you

After the chag
I will text you
After the chag
I will talk you
After the chag
I will see you
After the chag

After the chag
I will … you
After the chag

New York, October 16, 2016

---

[18] *Chag sameach*: Happy holiday (*chag* = holiday in Hebrew).

Share a poem

I know we should talk
But I am afraid to do so
No engagement you said
We could talk and still see other people
You said

Difficult for me
I get caught up when I start talking
Even more than when I text
And then if I start liking you
There will be no place for others
Till we finally meet
And I will know then
In the first few minutes
If you and I have a chance

You see, we did not even talk
But I was wondering if we actually did
When I thought of you during the prayers
I thought I would text you
After the holiday
Share a poem or two
Despite the danger

Please don't let me
Please
Don't let me think of you

New York, September 23, 2017

Contained fire

I

Just meeting a new guy for a date
And for two and a half hours
Sitting and standing close to him
With my modest skirt
In a big *shul*
Without talking to each other
But glancing at him briefly
Through the gaps of the *mechitza*[19]
And listening to his voice singing
And then being called at the Torah
Because they will call you
And what is he going to think of me
Does he find me pretty
Because he knows I am smart
But will he be interested in me
Isn't that a good way to start low and go slow
Through the respectful intimacy of praying near each other
As if you think that I would not be distracted during the service
If you are waiting for it to finish in order to finally see me

II

And here it comes again
That pinch in the heart
And here again will I
Be waiting for more time
To hear his voice

---

[19] Separation between men and women in a synagogue

And to see if that voice
Matches the words he wrote
Or maybe more

            III

Maybe this is it
Who knows
But don't believe in it
Because you have been disappointed
But this time it is different
For sure
And what if for a change

It is not anymore a pinch in my heart
But the sound of a thunder
Like a barely contained fire
Like a candle burning from both sides
Is it serious, Doctor?
Is it believable, Rabbi?

I am dreading and yearning at the same time
The first 30 seconds when we will see each other
Will there be a spark?
Or will it be like the sharp pain from a candle
You extinguish with your fingers?

New York, June 6, 2017

Mechitza

Like a veil of mystery
Wrapping your face
Out of sight

Like a first kiss through the veil
A kiss to build a dream on
Out of touch

Through the *mechitza*
I will peek at you

With holy thoughts
Of *Kabbalat Shabbat*
Boi kallah
Shabbat Malketa
Enter, bride
Sabbath Queen

Hitorreri Hitorreri
Arise Arouse
Ori Uri
My light My skin

Yasis Alayich
Elokaich
Kimsos Chatan
Al kallah

May your God rejoice
On you
Like a groom would
On his bride

New York, November 18, 2016
Thanks to Shlomo Halevi Alkabetz: "Lechah Dodi," 1579

Without love

Without love I will wake up
Say good morning to you, go to the bathroom brush my teeth
Help the kids to get ready to school, take a shower
Pray, go to work

Without love I will come back in the evening
And say: "Honey I am home"
Without love you will smile at me

Without love, I will ask the kids what they have done
Play with them, help them with their homework, have dinner
Without love, I will do the dishes, clean up the table
Put them to bed, read them a story, brush their teeth

Without love, I will ask you about your day
Go to bed, read a bit, watch TV, or work with the computer
Without love you will read your book
Without love, I may give you a massage or go to sleep
Without love, I may make love to you, without love, without love
Or I may be not
Without love I will say good night

Without love, I will wake up
In the middle of the night, without love
Without love, I will look at you asleep
With your face on your pillows and your leg on the sheets

And I will remember
That one time
You loved me, without love, without love, without love

New York, August 28, 2006

Avi

Il a trouvé une boite Dans le sable. Il a jeté une poignée de sable Dans la boite. Tout seul.	He found a box In the sand. He threw a handful of sand In the box. All alone.

Il a trouvé une boite
Dans le sable.
Il a jeté une poignée de
    sable
Dans la boite.
Tout seul.

Il a trouvé le couvercle de
    la boite
Dans le sable.
Avec le couvercle,
Il a versé du sable
Dans la boite.
Tout seul.
En me regardant.

Il a fermé
La boite pleine de sable
Avec le couvercle.
Tout seul.
Sans un mot.
En me regardant.
Et il me l'a donnée.

Alors, debout
Dans le bac à sable,
Au milieu des parents,
J'ai mis ma main sur mes
    yeux
Et j'ai pleuré.

He found a box
In the sand.
He threw a handful of
    sand
In the box.
All alone.

He found the cover of the
    box
In the sand.
With the cover,
He poured sand
In the box.
All alone.
While looking at me.

He closed
The box full of sand
With its cover.
All alone.
Without a word
While looking at me.
And he gave it to me.

Then I, standing
In the sandbox
Among all the parents,
I put my hand over my
    eyes
And I cried.

New York, April 10, 2005
English translation from the original French
Homage to Jacques Prévert: Déjeuner du matin, Paroles, *1946*

6 Relationships
A Psychiatrist's Narrative
141-147

Relationships: A psychiatrist's narrative

This essay analyzes the relationships and interactions between the observing narrator and the people he observed, as described in two stories of this collection: ***In a cloud of smoke*** and ***The melody***. After reviewing the characteristics of those relationships, we will uncover the implied model used during the interactions between observer and observed. We will draw the implication that this model has for the practice of psychotherapy and psychiatry, especially when using narratives as a therapeutic tool.

The narrator of ***In a cloud of smoke***, along with other staff members, participates in a symbolic burial ceremony at the end of a program at the National Center for Post-Traumatic Stress Disorder (PTSD) at West Haven VA Hospital in 1992. This ceremony occurs towards the end of a hospitalization of a group of Vietnam War veterans who were treated there together for several weeks. During their hospitalization, each veteran would process the specific traumatic events that affected them. Each Veteran had told his own story, which had been shared with the other members of the group. They received support from each other and from their families while expressing their personal narrative. In preparation for the ceremony, which was well attended by their families or loved ones, the veterans were asked to write a list of the fallen soldiers they were mourning. This ceremony was meant to help the veterans to have closure for their losses. The ritual has been described by David R. Johnson, who was directing that program at the time.[1]

The narrative of ***In a cloud of smoke*** is written from the point of view of a psychiatrist who had just joined that program and participated initially as a newcomer and a stranger, and in the chorus of treatment staff in the mourning ceremony. During that ceremony, as in another ceremony (the "crossing over" ceremony commemorating the program's completion), the staff chorus repeats comforting lines intended to heal the veterans from their trauma and foster the connection and integration with their families and communities. With words like "we let you down" or "this is war," the chorus tries to repair the feeling of abandonment that the veterans experienced when they returned from war. The input of the staff chorus in this ritual was also supposed to alleviate the veterans' burden of guilt for having survived their fellow soldiers in this brutal war involving dangerous enemies and innocent civilians. Ultimately, at the end of the mourning ceremony, the staff chorus, acting as a moral court, authorizes the veterans to release the spirits of the fallen soldiers they were holding onto and that prevented the veterans from moving back into civilian life.

The ritual created by Johnson, the Master of Ceremonies in this story, has an implied religious overtone, using Christian symbols, such as the crown of thorns worn by Christ, and the Hindu ritual of cremation. These Christian and Hindu rituals are foreign to the narrator's tradition and contribute to his discomfort and sense of distance. Bilu and Witztum, respectively an anthropologist and a psychiatrist in Israel, describe several interesting uses of religious-like rituals in psychiatric practice, in a more culturally competent approach for their Orthodox Jewish patients[2]. It is obviously more difficult to be culturally specific in a more multicultural group setting, such as in our story. Johnson describes previous homecoming rituals inspired by Native American rituals, adapted for Vietnam veterans[21]. Those rituals did not match the cultural perspective of most veterans and therefore Johnson advocated the use of different, "more secular" rituals. However, in his ritual, which is called the *Ceremony for the Dead* as described in our story, spirituality and religion are still very present, even if only implied.

In *In a cloud of smoke*, when the psychiatrist is exposed to this intense mourning ritual, he confronts his own past and his own narrative. The broken narrative of the veterans and the healing narrative of the chorus sometime clash with the psychiatrist's own narrative. At a certain point, the psychiatrist became aware that his narrative interferes with his experience of the ceremony. The psychiatrist views the list of the names of fallen soldiers as a sacred writing. Its burning is perceived as sacrilegious, like the burning of a Torah scroll during the Roman persecutions, or like the burning of Jews and others in the crematorium at Auschwitz. The psychiatrist then sees for a brief instant the burning spirits detaching from each name of the fallen soldiers' list, flying off in a cloud of smoke. This almost hallucinatory experience dramatically expresses the narrator's discomfort. On one hand, he feels connected to the veteran's narrative involving the spirits of the fallen soldiers. On the other hand, he also connects with the ancient and disturbing Talmudic story of a rabbi wrapped in a Torah scroll and burned alive by the Romans. In that narrative, the Talmud reports that the rabbi said before dying: "I see the parchment being consumed but the letters are flying off and they remain.[3]"

Ultimately, the narrator overcomes his discomfort and accepts the ceremony rituals when he sees the veterans' intense concentration and emotions. For them, the burning of the sheet carrying the names of their lost comrades is not a religious sacrilege, but is full of meaning. In the *Hasidic Tales of the Holocaust*[4], the Grand Rabbi of Bluzhov was able to light the first flame of a makeshift Hanukkah candleholder while imprisoned in the Bergen-Belsen concentration camp. After reciting the first two traditional blessings, the Rabbi doubted if he could continue with the third blessing thanking God "who made us live to reach this time"[5] while hundreds of dead Jewish bodies were lying literally within the shadow of the Hanukkah lights. Then he noticed the attention of the simple Jews who, despite death lurking in every corner, expressed their faith and devotion as they participated in this ritual. The Rabbi then could recite that third blessing, thanking God for witnessing a people with such faith and fervor. Here too, at the Vietnam Veteran Memorial, the intense emotions of the veterans overcome the problematic burning of the names and make it acceptable to the psychiatrist, considering the circumstances. This connection between the simple devotion of the surviving concentration camp inmates, and the intense suffering of the survivors of the Vietnam War, helps the narrator to empathize and deeply relate to the veterans.

This mourning ritual elicited strong reactions from the narrator and reactivated his grief related to the Holocaust. Because the narrator psychiatrist becomes aware of his own feelings and of his own narrative, he can better relate to and absorb the narrative of the hospitalized Veterans.

Narratives have been used in therapy to help patients deconstruct their problem-saturated stories and create an alternate, empowering story. The therapist acts as a catalyst in this process. Gardner and Poole describe narrative therapy as follow:

> "A postmodern approach to the practice and theory of therapeutic counseling, narrative therapy is a collaborative process predicated on the belief that identity is cocreated in social, cultural, and political contexts and revealed through stories and narratives. Narrative therapy involves unearthing dominant or 'problem' stories in people's lives (i.e., 'the addiction story'), understanding them, and retelling them in alternative and more empowering ways."[6]

Narratives have also been used in order to try to master and ultimately alleviate traumatic memories[7]. Some have criticized this approach and said that the therapist's own narrative may interfere in this process.[8] In order to avoid that pitfall, therapists have to articulate their own narrative, as in this story, while eliciting a therapeutic narrative from a patient.

In *The melody*, as in *In a cloud of smoke*, the narrator attempts initially to be an impartial participant and observer in a religious or semi-religious ritual. However, in *The melody* this attempt clearly fails and the narrator, in observing the outside reality, end up changing it. The narrator comes as an observer (or even a "voyeur") and finishes by being himself observed by the Hasidim and in turn, affecting them. This description corresponds to a postmodernist approach to relationships, far from the positivist approach in which there is clear separation between the observer and the reality being observed. Wolff-Michael Roth, while discussing the postmodern use of autobiography in auto-ethnography, summarizes this postmodernist approach:

> "The idea of an independence of the observer (and therefore his/her knowledge) and the world observed has been seriously questioned both in the natural and the social sciences. In the natural sciences, relativity theory and quantum mechanics both suggest that the status of the observer codetermines what and how it is observed. (...) The observer and the observed cannot be separated, and if what and how the observer perceives is determined by the current state of the organism that has its history. (...) In human terms, this requires us a better understanding of the autobiography of the individual observer."[9]

Assuming this interdependence between observer and observed, the analysis of the interaction between the therapist and the patient becomes an essential treatment tool for certain schools of psychotherapy such as Relational Psychoanalysis[10], Transference Focused Psychotherapy[11], and Intersubjectivity Therapy:

> Intersubjectivity theory is based on the premise that both the client and the therapist bring something of themselves and of their respective past emotional experience to the therapeutic relationship. This theoretical orientation is very attentive to the dynamics in the therapy room, especially of the relationship

> between therapist and client. It attends to how the client and the psychotherapist interact with each other, as well as how they feel about each other, consciously and subconsciously.[12]

During psychotherapy, the patient can interact even unconsciously with the therapist. The observation and awareness of the relationship between the therapist and the patient is necessary in order to maintain appropriate boundaries between them, while helping therapists understand the inner feeling of their patients. Sometimes a therapist is able to experience her patient's emotions, when the patient uses the defense mechanism of projective identification[13]. For example, the patient could project his own feeling of incompetence onto his therapist and may unconsciously try to make her feel incompetent instead of him. By understanding this process, the therapist can determine the patient's real feelings about himself despite his superior and devaluating demeanor. Therapists need to understand their own defense mechanism in order to sort out whether their feelings come from their own issues or if those feelings are imposed on them by the patient. This is one reason why psychoanalysts are required to undergo psychoanalysis prior to providing therapy.

We saw how the psychiatrist developed his own narrative when observing the collaborative narrative of veterans and staff. As illustrated in the two stories, we too can apply more broadly the model of interactive narratives between the observer and the observed. Narrative therapists need to take this model into account, to be conscious of our own personal narratives and to be aware of how they may interact with and relate to the narrative of their patients.

NOTES for *Relationships: A psychiatrist's narrative*

[1] Johnson, D.R., Feldman, S.C,. Lubin. H. and Southwick, S.M. (1995). The therapeutic use of ritual and ceremony in the treatment of post-traumatic stress disorder. *Journal of Traumatic Stress.* Apr;8(2):283–98.

[2] Bilu, Y. and Witztum, E. (1993). Working with Jewish ultra-orthodox patients: guidelines for a culturally sensitive therapy. *Culture, Medicine, and Psychiatry.* 1993 Jun;17(2):197–233.

[3] Babylonian Talmud, *Avodah Zarah*, 18a.

[4] Eliach, Y. (ed.) (1982). *Hasidic Tales of the Holocaust.* New York: Oxford University Press, pp. 13–15

[5] The *shehecheyanu* blessing in Hebrew.

[6] Gardner, P. and Poole, J. (2009). One story at a time: narrative therapy, older adults, and addictions." *Journal of Applied Gerontology.* 28: 600–620.

[7] Schauer, M., Neuner, F., and Elbert, T. (2011). *Narrative Exposure therapy: A Short-term Treatment for Traumatic Stress Disorders* (2nd revised and expanded edition). Cambridge, MA: Hogrefe Publishing.

[8] Meier, S. T. (2012). *Language and Narratives in Counseling and Psychotherapy.* Springer Publishing Company, p. 93.

[9] Roth, W-M. (2005). Auto/biography and Auto/ethnography: finding the generalized other in the self. In: *Auto/Biography and Auto/Ethnography: Praxis of Research Method*, Wolff-Michael Roth (ed.) Sense Publishers.

[10] Aron, L. (1991). The patient's experience of the analyst's subjectivity. In: S. Mitchell and L. Aron (eds.), *Relational Psychoanalysis: The Emergence of a Tradition.* 1999: Hillsdale, NJ: Analytic Press, pp. 243–268.

[11] Kernberg, O.F.; Yeomans, F.E.; Clarkin, J.F. and Levy, K.N. (2008). Transference focused psychotherapy: Overview and update. *International Journal of Psycho-Analysis* 89:601–620

[12] Larson, J, S. (2005). *Relational Aspects of Intersubjectivity Therapy and Gestalt Therapy:* A Theoretical Integration. (Doctoral dissertation, Pacific University, p. 3.) Retrieved from: http://commons.pacificu.edu/spp/4

[13] Ogden, H. P. (1979). On projective identification. *International Journal of Psycho-Analysis*, 60: 267–268. Retrieved from: https://pdfs.semanticscholar.org/303e/20a9ec17de0b6f7d49ed466faca9090d4e13.pdf

7 Original writings in French and Hebrew

Paris

The melody   151-153
The device   155-162
The revolt   163-164
Lena   165-166

New in America

New in town   167-168
In a cloud of smoke   169-172
Let's go, children   173-175
The last leaf   177
Word's cemetery   179
A pink short coat   181-182
We will be back   183-184

Jerusalem

Insh'Allah (God willing)   185-186

La mélodie (The melody)

Le Rabbi avait demandé à Ron d'entonner la chanson suivante. Non, ce n'était pas possible. Ron était là en observateur, en tant que voyeur. Et il observait : les quinze ou vingt Hassidim assis autour de la table avaient tourné leur regard vers lui en attendant gentiment que Ron s'exécute. Non. Ron ne se sentait pas digne de cet honneur. Il percevait sur sa chair la pression du porte-monnaie dans la poche arrière de son pantalon. Lorsque Ron était arrivé à Budapest, il avait cherché à assister un Chabat à un « troisième repas » célébré par les Hassidim. Il s'était dit qu'en retournant au pays d'origine il aurait une vision plus authentique de la vie hassidique d'après-guerre.

Ron avait été pris de court, surpris d'apprendre que des Hassidim se réunissaient encore, en 1977. Yanosh, un étudiant de l'école rabbinique –non hassidique– (la seule école rabbinique dans les pays de l'Est à l'époque) avait accepté de lui servir de guide. Il lui avait montré le chemin, mais n'était pas entré dans l'immeuble. Evidemment, Yanosh désapprouvait le mode de vie des Hassidim, mais il comprenait la curiosité de Ron.

Il n'avait pas eu le temps de se changer et avait dû conserver son porte-monnaie dans son pantalon, malgré l'interdiction du Chabat. Il était le seul étranger dans la petite salle de la synagogue. Les hommes présents avaient tous au moins la soixantaine passée. L'atmosphère n'était pas hostile. A l'exception du Rabbi, ils étaient tous sans barbe et aucun ne portait les vêtements traditionnels des Hassidim, si bien que Ron voulu s'assurer qu'on allait chanter les chansons hassidiques. Un homme lui répondit « bien sûr », d'un air protecteur comme à un jeune novice.

Ron avait attendu ce moment. Dans sa tournée de l'Europe de l'Est, il n'avait prévu que trois jours à Budapest, mais il s'était arrangé qu'un de ces jours soit un Chabat. Il voulait être le témoin du légendaire enthousiasme qui s'emparait des Hassidim durant le « troisième repas », juste avant la fin de la tombée de la nuit. Ils désiraient peut-être par leurs chants pleins de ferveur, prolonger pour encore quelques instants ce moment déjà nostalgique qui ne se renouvellerait qu'après une semaine d'attente.

L'office de l'après-midi précédait le fameux « repas ». Ron alla s'assoir sur un des bancs avec les autres. L'office avait été expédié par routine, et le Rabbi vêtu d'un caftan noir délivra un sermon en Yiddish. Il semblait fatigué de réciter son monologue. Les Hassidim écoutaient sagement en attendant la fin. L'office terminé, tous se dirigèrent vers la longue table en bois rustique, située vers l'entrée de la pièce. Le Rabbi s'assit en bout de table, et Ron qui avait retrouvé l'homme qui l'avait accueilli, s'était placé à ses côtés. Le « repas » se composait principalement de pain et de hareng mariné.

Et les Hassidim se mirent à chanter.

Ron n'avait jamais entendu rien de pareil. Les têtes dodelinantes récitaient une mélodie inconnue. Les notes de musique étaient là, et les paroles aussi. Le hareng était là, et la table, et la synagogue, et les Hassidim rasés, et le Rabbi fatigué. Mais la mélodie avait disparu, ici aussi, même dans le pays ancien.

Ron voyait des fantômes, des survivants, des vieillards répétant des rites d'antan, déjà fossilisés. Le Rabbi qui avait dû remarquer qu'il suivait les paroles, s'adressa pour la première fois à Ron, et lui demanda de chanter. Le porte-monnaie le brûlait presque, mais Ron ne pouvait pas refuser.

Le premier couplet, Ron le récita seul. Le voisin qui l'avait pris sous son aile s'écarta légèrement, et lui donna du coude. Il murmura avec un étonnement teinté de respect, sur un ton de confidence de la part d'un initié : « Mais, c'est hassidique ! »

Ron fut surpris d'entendre certains Hassidim entonner avec lui le deuxième couplet alors qu'ils essayaient d'apprendre la mélodie, évidemment nouvelle pour eux. Puis ce fut toute la communauté qui chanta. Les Hassidim semblaient se réveiller d'une longue torpeur. Certains esquissaient un sourire, comme s'ils venaient de réaliser qu'ils n'étaient plus seuls au monde, comme s'il y avait là, dans le pays nouveau qu'ils n'avaient jamais visité, des jeunes capables de reprendre et passer à leur tour le flambeau.

Ron était venu de Paris en quête d'une ancienne mélodie et il s'était trouvé en position de messager, insufflant la vie à une musique qui avait perdu son âme.

Le 25 mai 1992
New Haven, CT

LE BIDULE
(The device)

Quand il se releva, la petite sonnerie comme un réveil électrique s'infiltrait dans la nuit, sur le trottoir noir luisant après la pluie. En face de la porte au bord du trottoir, près de la chaussée se tenait quelqu'un, debout. Maxim avait l'impression qu'elle l'attendait, et qu'elle allait même lui adresser la parole quand le téléphone se mit à sonner. « Allo ? Est-ce que vous pourriez… ? » Et le patron lui expliqua ce qui venait de se passer en précisant que d'après lui, le client ne devrait pas tarder à se monter. Maxim n'avait pas eu le temps d'être fâché d'avoir été interrompu dans la rencontre avec sa visiteuse, car sur le moment il l'avait presque oubliée. Cependant Maxim avait l'impression qu'il venait de se passer quelque chose et il essayait maintenant de se remémorer les derniers instants précédant le coup de téléphone.

Le vendeur était comme d'habitude dans le magasin (une sorte de parfumerie ou quelque chose du genre) quand le téléphone se mit à sonner. « Allo ? Est-ce que vous avez un… ? » et le client se mit à lui décrire une sorte de bidule bien compliqué qui aurait pu avoir la consistance du plastique avec une forme allongée en spirale un peu comme un petit escargot mais pas exactement. « Mais non, vous devez faire erreur nous ne faisons pas ça.» « Alors quelle est l'adresse du magasin s'il vous plait ? » Le vendeur la lui donna après un moment de surprise, sans penser à mal et sans s'être demandé comment un client pouvait connaitre le numéro de téléphone et non l'adresse. Mais une fois qu'il eut raccroché il fut pris d'une espèce de remords, et sans très bien comprendre

La première image qui lui revint fut ce trottoir luisant avec les lumières de la ville, puis la silhouette d'une personne habillée en sombre qui s'apprêtait peut-être à lui adresser la parole. Maxim ne se rappelait pas de la forme de ses vêtements ni de leur longueur. Il était probable cependant, que même s'ils avaient été un peu courts, ils auraient été portés sous un manteau ou un imperméable d'une longueur plus raisonnable. Maxim n'arrivait pas à se souvenir des mots qu'elle aurait pu prononcer. Il n'avait de toute façon pas le temps de s'occuper de ces balivernes car il devait s'habiller rapidement pour aller au magasin. Il était déjà trop en retard et il aurait bien le loisir d'y réfléchir dans le métro. Mais il avait peur que s'il attendait trop, sa mémoire s'évanouirait au point qu'il oublierait même de se remémorer ce qui s'était passé.

Maxim ne voulait surtout pas que le patron lui retéléphone pour le rappeler à l'ordre. En cinq ans de service cette mésaventure ne lui était arrivée qu'une fois. Il enfila son pardessus sans même avoir pris le temps d'avaler un café. Il affrontait déjà des visages à peine rafraichis et pour la plupart encore somnolents : ces visages souvent lourdement maquillés, qui semblaient eux aussi juste sortis des oreillers. Les odeurs douteuses s'entremêlaient aux parfums forts et au rouge à lèvres de ceux qui s'en allaient au travail. Le court trajet de métro (trop court aujourd'hui surtout) ne laissait pas à Maxim suffisamment de temps pour se remémorer sa visiteuse. Que s'était-il passé de si important ? Il lui semblait bien qu'ils avaient engagé une conversation. Il dévisageait discrètement les quelques jolies

pourquoi, il sentit qu'il venait de faire du tort à son patron. Il fit alors le numéro du patron et lui expliqua ce qui venait de se passer en précisant que d'après lui, le client ne devrait pas tarder à se montrer. Le patron entra brusquement dans le magasin quelques instants plus tard. Sans prendre le temps d'enlever son pardessus, il se précipita vers la vitrine et en retira une vulgaire boite de savon qui était exposée bien en vue, ce genre de boite en plastique ovale ou rectangulaire rose pâle ou bleu clair. Sans faire attention à ses employés, le patron ouvrit la petite boite par le milieu et en sortit le « bidule ». Le problème était maintenant de cacher la petite boite vide car elle aurait pu paraitre suspecte et donner un indice qui pourrait faire remonter jusqu'au… bidule. Sans perdre la moindre seconde le patron entra dans l'arrière-boutique. Il y avait là des boites en carton noires plus ou moins

têtes autour de lui, et il se surprit à essayer d'y reconnaitre le visage de sa visiteuse. Mais une des voyageuses ayant manifesté une impatience contenue envers sa petite inspection, il sortit son journal pour se donner bonne contenance. Ses yeux étaient accrochés aux gros titres de la première page pliée en quatre, mais son esprit se délectait à imaginer la rencontre avec la visiteuse. « Tu cherches quelqu'un ? » lui aurait-elle dit. Maxim se souvenait qu'il n'avait pas été surpris par cette question posée de façon si naturelle. En guise de réponse il avait dû prononcer des phrases banales qui ne le satisfaisaient pas vraiment. Mais à vrai dire, c'était peut-être lui qui avait posé la question. Cette fois-ci, Maxim fut fâché d'être tiré de sa rêverie pour

conversation. Il descendre à sa station de métro. Et c'est à ce moment-là qu'il s'aperçu qu'il avait

156

oublié la boite de savon en plastique. Il n'avait pas alors attaché trop d'importance à la demande du patron au téléphone, et puis ses idées n'étaient pas tout à fait claires Et ensuite, tout en étant pressé de s'habiller, il avait essayé de se souvenir de cette rencontre interrompue et il n'avait effectué que des gestes automatiques. Sans très bien comprendre pourquoi, il fut pris d'une espèce de remords et il sentit qu'il venait de faire du tort à son patron. Le magasin n'était déjà plus très loin, et il en apercevait la devanture. C'est à peine si Maxime avait pu remarquer un étonnement de la part des autres employés quand il les avait salués. Cela le rassurait un peu. Le vendeur reprit donc sa place habituelle en s'efforçant de ne rien laisser paraître, et il arrangeait la vitrine du magasin comme à l'accoutumée à cette heure de la journée, lorsqu'il lui sembla grandes qui contenaient des lots de parfum avec peut-être des savons de toilette ou des produits de beauté comme du rouge à lèvres, mais en tout cas il y avait surement des bouteilles de parfum plus ou moins grandes ou nombreuses suivant la dimension des boites en carton. Le patron choisit la plus grosse boite et déchira le couvercle proprement suivant le bord. Puis il sortit la grosse bouteille de parfum et peut-être quelques autres petites choses. Quand le fond de la boite en carton fut libéré il y posa la petite boite vide puis il remit dans l'ordre les petites choses puis la grosse bouteille et il rabattit le couvercle en carton. A ce moment même, le client entrait dans le magasin, Peut-être redemanda-t-il le bidule mais dans l'hypothèse où il le fit, le patron lui-même aurait bien fait remarquer qu'ici c'était une parfumerie et qu'on ne vendait pas ça dans une parfumerie. De tout façon ce qui est sûr, c'est que le *que quelque chose manquait dans la vitrine. Le vendeur cherchait de quel objet il pouvait bien s'agir quand le téléphone se mit à sonner. « Allo ? Est-ce que vous avez un... ? » et le client se mit à lui décrire une sorte de bidule bien compliqué qui aurait pu avoir la consistance du plastique avec une forme allongée en spirale. « Il n'ait pas sûr que nous l'ayons en magasin, car il doit s'agir d'un modèle assez ancien. Mais nous pourrions en commander. »*
C'était encore un de ces coup de téléphone de routine auquel le vendeur était habitué, mais cette fois Maxim avait eu comme une impression fugitive de « déjà vu ». Peut-être avait-il déjà entendu cette voix. Il saisit l'opportunité d'une livraison pour emmener avec lui la jeune vendeuse stagiaire sous le regard ironique mais discret de la caissière. Maxim sonna à la porte correspondant à l'adresse de la

cliente en regardant vers la camera située au-dessus. La porte s'ouvrit électroniquement et Maxim se fit précéder par la jeune vendeuse. Ils pénétrèrent dans une sorte de sas se terminant par deux portes. Au-dessus était écrit en grands caractères : SECURITE. Sur la porte de gauche était inscrit le mot: FEMMES ; et sur l'autre: HOMMES. La vendeuse se tourna vers Maxim, pour vérifier qu'il n'y avait pas de danger, mais il lui expliqua qu'il valait mieux se plier aux règles de sécurité. Après avoir pénétré seul dans un petit hall, Maxim se trouva face à une hôtesse d'accueil assise derrière un guichet en verre. Elle était chargée de prendre les effets personnels du nouveau venu que celui-ci devait ranger sur un cintre, et lui remettre en échange un bracelet numéroté en plastique rouge, ainsi que le règlement complet de la

client demanda du parfum. Le vendeur qualifié présenta les différents articles en insistant sur l'avantage des lots. Le client demanda un lot du format le plus grand. Le vendeur qualifié entra dans l'arrière-boutique sous l'œil satisfait du patron. Le vendeur chercha les lots de grand format mais il n'en restait plus qu'un. Il sortit le présenter au client pour l'emballer comme il se doit. A ce moment-là le patron s'aperçut que le couvercle de la boite en carton présentait une déchirure. Il arracha le paquet et sous un prétexte quelconque fila dans l'arrière-boutique en passant devant le caissier dont le sourire ironique mais discret prouvait qu'il voyait bien son manège depuis le début. Le patron ouvrit le couvercle de la grosse boite en carton noire, en sortit la grande bouteille de parfum, sortit la petite boite vide puis il glissa la bouteille de parfum dans l'espace étroit qui lui était réservé dans la boite en

maison. Quand Maxim s'exécuta, l'hôtesse actionna l'ouverture d'une porte et il entra dans ce qu'il crut comprendre être une salle d'attente ou un salon d'observation. La pièce, de taille moyenne, rectangulaire, était dépourvue de tout mobilier à l'exception d'un banc moderne, formé d'une petite poutrelle en métal sur laquelle étaient soudées 5 ou 6 sièges sans pieds; ce genre de banc qu'on peut trouver dans la salle d'attente d'un hôpital. Mais, chose curieuse, il n'y avait pas de table basse sur laquelle on dispose habituellement quelques revues pour faire patienter les malades. Maxim choisit de s'assoir sur le siège fixé en dedans d'un des sièges occupant l'extrémité du banc, mais il évita tout de même de s'assoir sur les sièges centraux. Bien qu'il n'y ait ni fenêtre ni miroir (qui *aurait pu être sans tain)*, Maxim pensait qu'il était observé, et tout en essayant d'agir naturellement il cherchait à se montrer sous son jour le plus favorable. Il était un peu gêné par son absence de vêtement, mais bien moins que s'il n'avait pas été seul dans la pièce. Il n'y avait pas d'odeur perceptible, et la pièce était assez fortement éclairée du plafond, probablement par des néons. On n'entendait pas de bruit particulier, ni même ceux de la rue qui devait pourtant être toute proche. Maxim n'avait plus sa montre, qu'on lui avait prise à l'entrée, et aucune horloge n'était accrochée aux murs. Pour compter le temps, Maxim eut un moment l'idée de prendre son pouls. Cependant la méthode n'était pas très fiable, son pouls pouvant varier tout au cours de la journée. Maxim le savait bien car il avait consulté un médecin pour ce genre de problème, mais tout était rentré dans l'ordre. Bien que cela ne l'ait pas frappé en entrant dans la pièce,* carton noire puis il referma le couvercle et rendit le paquet au client qui sortit. Le patron eut alors envie de tout expliquer à ses employés mais déjà ceux-ci chahutaient comme des enfants et deux d'entre eux, même, sortaient du magasin bras dessus bras dessous comme si de rien était. Ils étaient déjà un peu loin quand le patron du sortir du magasin et les appeler en criant. Mais ils l'ignoraient totalement. Ce cri du patron eut l'air d'avoir de l'effet car ils rentrèrent, mais avec une pointe d'arrogance vis-à-vis du patron qui se sentait, lui, le vaincu de cette affaire. Mais comme il avait décidé de s'expliquer devant ses employés et que ceux-ci folâtraient dans tous les coins du magasin il énonça : « Tout le monde a la réunion au 5ème étage. (C'était peut-être le 6ème ou le 7ème mais surement pas le 4ème.) Il avait pris un ton détaché comme s'il ne s'agissait que d'une de ces réunions de routine où tout le monde est bien assis *imprécis, et il avait du mal à trouver le bon endroit. Maxim n'arrivait plus à concentrer sa pensée diffuse et il se*

Maxim trouvait à présent qu'il faisait un peu chaud, sans pour autant qu'il en arrive à transpirer. Il pensa qu'il serait plus sage de rester assis sur son siège car une tentative d'ouvrir l'une des deux portes serait probablement mal interprétée, et pourrait se retourner contre lui. De toute façon, il était plus que probable que ces portes elles aussi ne pouvaient s'ouvrir que commandées de l'extérieur et probablement électroniquement comme la porte d'entrée. Progressivement, Maxim trouva que son esprit se brouillait, que sa tête était lourde, que son cœur battait de plus en plus vite. Il essaya de se prendre le pouls comme le lui avait appris son médecin, mais son geste était

159

trompait lors du compte des pulsations, si bien que quand il s'arrêtait il ne se souvenait plus du tout du chiffre précédent. Il transpirait maintenant abondamment. Il fut pris de vertige et il se sentit si faible que, malgré son effort pour rester assis bien sagement sur son siège, il glissa tout doucement et se retrouva par terre près du banc. Maxim tenait encore, froissée dans sa main crispée, la feuille du règlement qu'on lui avait remise à l'entrée mais il ne s'en rendait plus compte. Quelques images se bousculaient dans sa tête puis s'évanouissaient sans qu'il puisse en contrôler le déroulement.

Maxim revoyait le sourire ironique mais discret de la caissière quand il était sorti du magasin, le regard impatient de la voyageuse du métro, le moment où il descendait la rue avec sa visiteuse et où il repensait à sa réponse

sagement sur sa chaise. Mais les employés s'amusaient vraiment beaucoup. En jouant à chat ou à cache-cache et en courant dans tous les sens ils se précipitèrent sans attendre le patron, dans l'unique ascenseur. Certains prirent peut-être l'escalier de secours à moins que ce ne fussent ceux qui étaient déjà arrivés par l'ascenseur qui continuaient leurs jeux dans l'escalier. De toute façon, le patron se retrouva seul dans le magasin et quand il arriva devant l'ascenseur une petite sonnerie comme un réveil électrique perçait à travers les rires et les bruits des employés qui descendaient et remontaient l'escalier de secours. Le patron leva la tête pour voir sur le tableau de chiffres lumineux en haut de la porte à quel étage était l'ascenseur. Mais à la place des chiffres il y avait une inscription lumineuse clignotante: DANGER (peut-être y avait-il écrit « attention, danger ») PANNE (peut-être ce mot-là n'était pas vraiment

qui ne l'avait pas vraiment satisfait. Maxim revoyait la jeune vendeuse qu'il avait emmenée avec lui, et c'est alors, essayant de repandre la direction de ses idées, qu'il se demanda ce qui avait bien pu lui arriver à elle aussi. C'était pourtant lui qui l'avait faite rentrer dans l'immeuble et elle l'avait suivi. Toujours dans le brouillard, Maxim crut voir un médecin se pencher sur lui. Il entendit comme un brouhaha de paroles autour de lui et il crut comprendre qu'on avait fouillé ses affaires et qu'on n'y avait pas trouvé la moindre identification, tandis que la voix de la jeune vendeuse disait qu'ils étaient venus pour une livraison. Maxim entendit vaguement

délibérer autour de lui. Ne connaissant pas sa religion, on avait résolu d'appeler un prêtre et un rabbin. Ceux-ci se *consultèrent et il fut décidé que dans le doute, on ne lui donnerait pas l'extrême-onction et on ne réciterait pas le kaddich. Maxim fit un effort terrible pour se concentrer et pour empêcher ses idées de fuir les unes à la suite des autres, et il déploya son ultime énergie à s'accrocher à la première image venue. Ce fut celle de l'hôtesse d'accueil qui lui revint. Quand il était dans le hall il ne semblait pas à Maxim qu'il avait regardé l'hôtesse avec précision, cependant des éléments revenaient dans sa mémoire avec un degré d'exactitude qui l'étonnait lui-même. L'hôtesse était assise à un bureau étroit, presque carré, dans une cage de verre, et on pouvait voir ses pieds à travers la vitre. Les pieds du bureau étaient constitués de tubes métalliques noirs très légèrement coniques. Chacun portait un embout de caoutchouc noir mat. L'hôtesse était assise sur une sorte de chaise haute en cuir noir (ou en skaï, on ne savait pas) dont le petit dossier lui arrivait au niveau des reins, l'obligeant à*

inscrit mais ça se pourrait bien) UNE FAUTE A ETE COMMISE (ou une autre phrase de ce genre). Ce n'était pas très clair. Qui avait commis cette faute? Mais on pouvait supposer que c'étaient les employés qui en jouant avaient déclenché cette panne. Du coup, le patron n'eut plus envie de rien expliquer aux employés, mais surtout il avait peur que ceux-ci restent dans le magasin à courir de tous les côtés car il savait qu'il ne pourrait pas les obliger à sortir. Il fut très soulagé de voir que les employés ne manifestaient aucunement l'envie de rester sur les lieux mais plutôt de gambader dehors comme avaient fait les deux premiers avant qu'il ne les rappelle. Quand tous les employés furent sortis, le patron sortit à son tour et ferma la serrure de la porte vitrée, au ras du sol.

UTRICULE
…

BIDULE

creuser le dos pour s'assoir bien droite. A l'extérieur, le brouhaha semblait avoir diminué. Le médecin avait déjà dû partir. Il entendit le prêtre et le rabbin délibérer, et pensant eux-aussi que Maxim avait fini son séjour ici-bas, ils décidèrent de partir à leur tour. La pièce devait se vider peu à peu et Maxim était probablement seul quand il se rappela la voix familière au téléphone, et dans un suprême effort, il articula des mots dont il ne connaissait pas même toujours l'existence et qu'il se surprenait à prononcer :

SACCULE…
VESICULE …
UTRICULE …

VESTIBULE
…

Dictionnaire Larousse :
Bidule : nom masculin (peut-être picard bidoule, boue)
Familier. Chose dont on ne sait pas exactement le nom ou qu'on ne tient pas à préciser davantage.
Populaire. Matraque de policier.
http://www.larousse.fr/dictionnaires/francais/bidule/9144?q=bidule#9067 (accédé le 12/31/17)

Dictionnaire de la langue française, par É. Littré :
Utricule : (u-tri-ku-l') s. m.
Renflement du labyrinthe membraneux de l'oreille
Saccule : (sa-ku-l') s. m.
Une des deux vésicules du vestibule membraneux de l'oreille moyenne, logée dans la fossette ronde vestibulaire. Le saccule communique avec l'autre vésicule et est tapissé d'otoconie.
Vestibule : (vè-sti-bu-l') s. m.
Cavité irrégulière qui fait partie de l'oreille interne.
Vésicule : (vé-zi-ku-l') s. f.
Terme didactique. Petite vessie, petite cavité ou poche.
https://www.littre.org/ (accédé le 12/31/17)

Paris, 1978 - 1985

La révolte (The revolt)

C'était l'heure du repas à la cantine d'une école primaire. Jamais Maurice ne se serait souvenu de cette cantine et de ses joyeux déjeuners si, pendant un certain repas, un grave incident n'avait troublé profondément le petit enfant insouciant qu'il était alors.

Maurice ne se rappelait pas ce qu'ils avaient mangé, ni si il avait faim ou non –il devait avoir faim-, ni quel âge il pouvait avoir. Tous ce dont il se souvenait, c'est qu'il était dans une des petites classes de l'école primaire et qu'il se trouvait par hasard, ou plutôt à cause de la surveillante, à une table de « grands ». Evidemment, de chaque plat, les « grands » prenaient toujours les plus grosses parts et lui laissaient la plus petite. C'était méchant, mais il ne pouvait rien dire. C'était normal.

Il se rappelait maintenant que c'était le printemps. Le soleil brillait. Les moineaux sifflaient gaiement dans les arbres de la cour. Il tournait le dos au soleil. Il diffusait doucement sa lumière sombre dans le grand réfectoire. Une mouche voletait de-ci de-là à travers les rires et les bavardages. Il la suivait des yeux. Elle était amusante. A côté de lui les grands se tordaient de rire, pliés en deux par une blague faite par l'un d'eux. La mouche avait l'air très contente, là-haut de les voir tous s'agiter ainsi. Elle avançait très lentement pour pouvoir tous les regarder plus longtemps chacun. Justement elle était au-dessus d'eux, près de la table.

Soudain, un des « grands » souleva un verre vide et emprisonna la grosse mouche contre la table. Il criait triomphalement : « Elle a bien le droit de mourir, non ! » Maurice sortit de ses gonds et lui répliqua d'un air lamentable : « Elle a aussi le droit de vivre ! » Il assistait ensuite, impuissant, à l'agonie de la grosse mouche. Les grands lui coupèrent les ailes et les pattes et finalement ils l'écrasèrent. Un frisson lui passa dans le dos. Les grands lui faisaient peur. Il se reculait. Il les voyait rire, fier de leur bravoure.

Maurice eut, tout à coup, l'envie de rester toujours petit. C'était absurde, bien-sûr, mais il ne voulait pas passer par cet âge attristant. Il revoyait la mouche écrasée, la folie des grands, leur bêtise. Peut-être les hommes sont-ils mauvais ? Donc il était mauvais. Non, il n'était pas mauvais : Il était un enfant, pas un homme. Il deviendrait mauvais. Il était désorienté, affolé par l'avenir. Il ne voulait pas devenir come les grands. Jamais. Mais, que faire ?

Paris, le 14 décembre 1971

Lena

Elle a été accompagnée par ses amis, venus de partout, de Boston au Sentier, par un après-midi d'hiver, gris et froid. Ils s'étaient rassemblés dans l'allée, par petits groupes, par famille, par cercle de connaissance. Ils auraient été contents de se retrouver, si ce n'était pas ici, en cette occasion.

«Attention», dit un homme plutôt grand, d'une voix forte et assurée, et qui semblait être en charge de la cérémonie. «Pour RoTenberg, c'est par là, pour RoZenberg, par ici » dit-il en accentuant la consonne différente. Et les proches de suivre la voiture sombre pour son dernier voyage, jusqu'à l'allée des peupleraies-peuplepleurait. Avec des gestes précis, l'homme sortit deux tabourets pliables, qu'il installa en face de la foule à une distance calculée l'un de l'autre. Puis du même ton impersonnel et professionnel, il invitât des volontaires à transporter Lena sur les tabourets. Un drapeau rouge-orange flétri, au tissu de velours râpé et discrètement déchiré vers le bas, enraidi à gauche par un mat comme on en voit pour les défilés des anciens combattants, fut posé à plat. Sur le drapeau était écrit simplement, en français uniquement, seule concession à la langue du pays d'accueil de Lena: «Cercle Amical», une traduction édulcorée de l'original yiddish «Arbeiter Ring», le cercle des travailleurs.

On aurait pu le prendre pour un Rabbin avec sa barbe rousse et blanche et sa casquette grisonnante à carreaux. Il parla de Lena en Yiddish uniquement, un Yiddish clair, que même les sépharades purent comprendre. Il parla de la petite Lena, de Lena la femme, la mère, l'intellectuelle polyglotte.

Un détail d'organisation avait dû échapper à la vigilance de Szulem son mari: probablement par routine respect pour la coutume juive, le maître de cérémonie à tête nue n'avait invité que des males à transporter Lena. Pourquoi? Lena, libre penseuse, faisant fi des traditions, et féministe avant la lettre, n'aurait-elle pas été fière d'avoir été portée à sa dernière demeure par au moins une femme?

New York, le 24 février 2005

חדש בעיר (New in town)

גרתי מספר שנים בניו יורק ומצאתי שם כמה מקצועות מוזרות, כמו צועד כלבים (דוג וולקער[20]) ומגן תינוק (בייבי פרופער[21]). למי שלא יודע, צועד הכלבים אוסף הרבה כלבים מבעליהם העסוקים והעשירים ומטייל אותם ברחובות. יש גם אולם התעמלות לכלבים (דוג ג'ים[22]) כדי שהכלבים יכולים להריח אחד את השני במקום סגור כשאינם נע ונד עם צועד הכלבים שלהם. מגן התינוק הוא בן אדם מבוגר שמעביר את זמנו זוחל על ארבע ורואה את העולם עם נקודת-מבט של תינוק שובב, וחושב באיזה מקום מרתק הוא יכול להכניס את אצבעותיו, למשל בשקע או תקוע בדלת הארון של ההורים. בשביל זה הוא מקבל סכר גבוה, לפי רמת הלימודים שלו.

כשהייתי חדש בעיר ועוד סטודנט שהגיע לאחרונה מפריז, מצאתי מקצוע שאף פעם לא שמעתי עליה מקודם. הייה לי רק תקציב קבוע ודק, וחסרו לי מכתב המלצה או תלוש משכורת. לכן חיפשתי מתוך פרסומת בעיתון חסידי ביידיש, מישהו שרצה להשכיר בלי שאלה סטודיו בזול לדייר משנה. הדירה הייתה בוויליאמסבורג בברוקלין, רק $5 במונית מגריניוויטש ווילאג'[23]. השכונה הייתה ענייה ולא יקרה אבל בטוחה, צירוף שלא הייה רגיל בתקופה הזו בעיר. בשכונה גרו הרבה חסידים מהונגריה, וכמעט כולם היו ניצולי שואה וצאצאיהם. באותו זמן בניו יורק הייה צריך להיזהר יותר על הביטחון; והאזור הייה כמו אי בטוח בקרב שכונות חשודות. גרתי בבניין ללא מעלית, קצת מקולקל ובלי שוער. לא היו לי הרבה חברים שהשכירו את דירתי, ולא ציפיתי אף אחד לבוא בלי הודעה. לכן הייתי מופתע כשיום אחד הפעמון צלצלה בלי אזהרה.

קודם כל חשבתי על הביטחון. הבטתי בחור הצצה בדלת, והסתכלתי באדם לובש מדים כחולים, אולי בגדי עבודה של פועל, שהייה מחכה בסבלנות. פתחתי את הדלת וראיתי אותו נושא בידו חפץ מתכתי, כמו מכשיר עם צוואר ארוך ורזה. "אני האקסטערמינאטור", הוא אמר. לא הבנתי את המילה אבל נדמתי לי שזה הייה שייך להשמדת היהודים בשואה שהרסה את אבותי ואת האבות של תושבי השכונה, למרות העמדה המנומסת של המשמיד הזה, שלא הייה מתנהג כמלאך המוות רגיל. הגיעו לי סמיכות מחשבות אחרות על המילה הזו: הייה עוד אפשר לראות ברחובות פרסומת של "הטערמינאטור" (הסרט הראשון) עם

---

[20] Dog walker
[21] Baby proofer
[22] Dog gym
[23] Greenwich Village

ארנולד שווארצנעגר והכתפיים העירומים והשרירים שלו, מחזיק מכונת ירייה גדולה מדי. חשבתי גם על הסרט היותר ישן של לויס בונועל, "המלאך המשמיד"[24]. מכל מקום, כל אסוציאציות האלו לא היו מרגיעות, וסגרתי במהירות את הדלת ומלמלתי: "תודה לא צריך".

עכשיו אני לא צוחק על המקצועות הללו והשמות המוזרים שלהם. להפך, אני מתחנן בפני המדביר שהוא יבוא לעתים יותר קרובות להרוס את הג'וקים שלי, וגם שילמתי המון בשביל יעוץ של מגן תינוק. ואם הייה לי כלב, מי יודע איזו עזרה הייתי מוכן לדרוש?

11 ספטמבר 2005

---

[24] El ángel exterminador (The exterminating angel) by Luis Buñuel

En fumée (In a cloud of smoke)

Les petites fleurs étaient en tissu. Les unes blanches comme pour un bouquet de mariée, les autres aux pétales rouges avec des feuilles vertes. La dame en imperméable parcourait les rangs des affligés et chacun choisissait une fleur rouge ou blanche. La fleur était ensuite tenue entre les doigts ou mise à la boutonnière.

Kalman regardait la mise en place d'une façon détachée, comme si ce qui se passait ne pouvait le toucher, comme s'il s'agissait d'un spectacle auquel il avait peu de part.

Il faisait froid. L'air était gris et Kalman avait été bien avisé de prendre son écharpe pour se protéger du vent.

« Serrez les rangs ». Le Maitre avait adressé cet ordre aux membres du chœur et il avait ouvert ses bras pour les regrouper. Kalman avait ressenti un mélange de surprise et de malaise. Pour justifier son obéissance, il s'était dit que cela le réchaufferait. Puis il avait souri intérieurement et continué à jouer le jeu. Il eut un instant la vison cocasse de lui-même coude à coude avec des inconnus sur un coin de pelouse déserte coincée entre une autoroute bruyante et une rive marécageuse.

La dame qui distribuait les fleurs quitta le groupe des affligés et se dirigea vers le chœur. Kalman eut encore un fugitif sentiment de malaise quand il se rendit compte qu'il était supposé prendre une fleur lui aussi. I devait choisir rapidement la couleur, mais décida de prendre la fleur à portée de main. A la réflexion, Kalman pensait que la rouge était plus jolie et plus réaliste, mais il était déjà trop tard, et il planta la tige dans sa boutonnière.

Kalman avait déjà éprouvé un similaire sentiment de malaise lorsqu'il avait assisté au Messie de Händel pour la première fois, et quand à sa surprise, la foule s'était levée pour le dernier morceau. Kalman les avait imités en expliquant qu'ainsi il pourrait mieux voir la scène. La deuxième fois, il s'était levé pour faire comme tout le monde, sans autre justification et sans trop être gêné d'honorer une religion qui avait persécuté ses ancêtres.

Le Maitre de cérémonie prononça quelques paroles fermes devant le monument de marbre noir en forme de « V ». Kalman regarda les Vétérans qui formaient le groupe des affligés. Certains portaient leurs insignes ou leurs décorations sur leurs casquettes ou sur leur blouson de cuir. Une femme et un jeune enfant confortaient un home d'une quarantaine d'années avec une natte. Puis fut lancé l'ordre de déposer les fleurs au pied du monument aux morts, chacun à son rythme. Sans un instant d'hésitation, l'homme à la natte fut le premier à s'exécuter.

Et d'attendre son tour, et de décider de n'aller ni trop tôt ni trop tard, et de s'approcher près du monument, et de se baisser, et de glisser la fleur dans la couronne de brindille de bois ressemblant à la couronne d'épines portée par le Christ souffrant. Et de retourner à sa place, et de se serrer à nouveau.

De toute façon, Kalman, contrairement à ce qu'il avait imaginé, n'avait pas pu garder sa fleur. Il ne regrettait plus maintenant de ne pas avoir choisi la fleur rouge, et il se trouvait un peu ridicule de l'avoir pensé. Quelques semaines plus tard, Kalman eu par hasard l'occasion de remarquer un panier rempli de paquets de bonbons emballés dans de la gaze verte. Apres avoir demandé l'autorisation d'en prendre un, il dénoua la tige de la fleur rouge en tissu qui fermait le petit paquet. Il lut la notice : « Fait par des handicapés, Vétérans du

Vietnam », et il jeta la fleur sans remarquer qu'elle était identique à celle qu'il avait convoitée auparavant.

La cérémonie continuait, et personne parmi l'assemblée ne semblait tout à fait sûr de son rôle. Sous la direction du Maitre de Cérémonie, le chœur formé par le personnel soignant répondait à l'unisson au groupe des Vétérans : « Nous vous autorisons à vous libérer des esprits des morts qui vous hantent depuis la guerre. Laissez ces esprits rejoindre les éléments naturels, la terre, le ciel et la mer et retrouvez votre paix intérieure. »

Un par un, les Vétérans s'approchaient d'un large vase en métal, et lisaient les noms des morts qui les hantaient, et le chœur du personnel répétait ces noms. Certains n'en donnaient pas, certains Vétérans en donnaient beaucoup ; un cita simplement « les gens sur le pont ». Que s'était-il passé sur ce pont ? On ne pouvait que trop deviner. Tous déposaient dans le vase, la feuille où étaient inscrit les noms, comme les Hasidim qui insèrent leur requête dans le mur des lamentations.

Puis le Maitre de Cérémonie mis le feu aux papiers dans l'urne et Kalman pu voir, l'espace d'un instant, les esprits brulés vifs se détacher des lettres de leur nom et s'envoler vers le ciel gris comme avait dû s'envoler la fumée des fours crématoires à Auschwitz. Kalman en voulu d'abord au Maitre d'avoir inventé cette partie du rituel, mais il se reprit rapidement devant la concentration et l'émotion des simples Vétérans.

Ensuite, la cendre devait être dispersée dans la mer comme dans les rites de deuil en Inde. Cependant Kalman ne put s'empêcher de penser au procès d'Eichmann et de ses cendres elles aussi dispersées dans la mer.

La fin de la cérémonie approchait : un trou fut creusé, le reste des cendres y fut dispersé et une fleur plantée. Les Vétérans et les soignants se tenaient la main en faisant un cercle autour de la fleur pour un moment de silence.

Voilà. Kalman avait participé à l'enterrement de morts qui n'étaient pas les siens. Peut-être était-il temps qu'il enterre ses morts lui aussi.

Le 22 janvier 1992
New Haven, CT

Allons z'enfants (Let's go, children)

Allons z'enfants de la patri-i-e...

La mélopée avait entouré Ben Gross, mais avec calme, comme si c'était une prière. Les paroles étaient nouvelles elles aussi. On était bien loin de cet hymne trop guerrier aux yeux de Gross. Et puis Gross n'avait pas vraiment la fibre patriotique pour son pays d'origine qui avait pu permettre la rafle du Vel d'hiv [25].

Doucement, comme un murmure venant des quatre coins de la salle, rythmé par le poing du Maitre sur l'estrade, les habitués chantaient avec sérieux et sans trop d'enthousiasme.

Le groupe des visiteurs se regarda au début de la chanson. Gross était maintenant un étranger depuis bien longtemps, et il avait perdu l'habitude de côtoyer ses compatriotes. Rien qu'à les observer Gross avait l'impression de les connaitre bien mieux que les autochtones. Il les regardait avec plaisir. Il était curieux de leur mode vestimentaire : Un seul avait endossé l'attirail complet des habitués, les autres portaient costume ou blouson ; Un semblait même à on aise dans son sweat-shirt qui vantait en français l'opération « Tempête dans le désert » ; Un autre encore, avec sa barbe de trois jours et son T-shirt noir sous la veste n'aurait pas détonné en boite de nuit le samedi soir. Gross imagina ce dernier s'habiller et choisir ce T-shirt noir qui, tout en faisant mode se mariait mieux avec le costume austère des habitués.

---

[25] La rafle du Vél'd'Hiv. A propos du film, voir :
http://www2.cndp.fr/TICE/teledoc/dossiers/dossier_rafle.htm

Les visiteurs étaient des gens simples, des commerçant pour la plupart, qui sentaient plus le mellah[26] que la France profonde, et Gross se dit qu'à Paris il n'avait pas l'habitude de s'identifier à eux.

Après un moment d'hésitation, les visiteurs, qui avaient été discrets pendant toute la durée du service, reprirent l'hymne avec fierté en lui donnant une énergie toute cocardière, comme si ce chant légitimait totalement leur présence dans la communauté. Et les habitués semblaient baisser le ton devant ce zèle inattendu.

Gross aussi était un visiteur. Il avait choisi de se mêler à ce groupe qu'il ne s'attendait pas à rencontrer. Il n'avait pas su qu'une soixantaine de personnes venaient tout exprès de Paris pour le weekend ; mais après avoir navigué dans la grande salle de la synagogue qui contenait bien deux à trois mille personnes, Gross avait fini par les remarquer. De plus, le groupe avait pris d'assaut le petit podium situé en arrière du Maitre, d'où on voyait la salle entière.

Allons z'enfants… Gross s'était mis à chanter avec une ardeur amusée, comme si lui aussi faisait partie du groupe. Il lui avait fallu, et Gross imaginait qu'il en était probablement de même pour les autres visiteurs, il lui avait fallu donc se déplacer à Brooklyn, à la grande cour du Rabbi de Loubavitch pour se réconcilier, pour un instant, pour un instant seulement, avec son hymne national. Il avait décidé de passer un Chabat à Crown Heights avec quelques amis de Manhattan et il avait trouvé la France, et un Paris qu'il croyait avoir oublié.[27]

---

[26] Mellah: Quartier Juif populaire dans les pays du Maghreb.
[27] Cette tradition Loubavitch de chanter l'air de la Marseillaise sur des paroles hassidiques a été instaurée en 1973 par le dernier Rabbi de Loubavitch afin de hâter la venue du messie. Déjà, et dans le même but, le premier Rabbi de Loubavitch avait converti une marche de l'armée impériale napoléonienne en chant hassidique. Voir la vidéo de ce chant :

Le 10 mai 1992
New Haven, CT

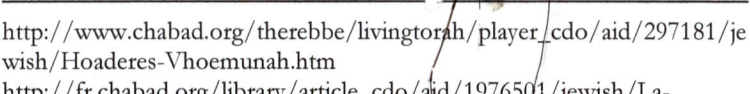

http://www.chabad.org/therebbe/livingtorah/player_cdo/aid/297181/jewish/Hoaderes-Vhoemunah.htm
http://fr.chabad.org/library/article_cdo/aid/1976501/jewish/La-Marseillaise-du-Rabbi.htm

La dernière feuille (The last leaf)

La dernière feuille de l'arbre
Est tombée
La dernière couleur de la rue
Jaune, rouge
Et six mois de ma vie

La dernière feuille de l'arbre
Va tomber
Et son jaune illumine la rue
Et ma vie

Le dernier jour de ma vie
A glissé
La dernière chaleur
Le denier regard
La dernière couleur

Le dernier jour de la vie
Va tomber
Et son regard illumine la rue
Et mon arbre
The last leaf of the tree
Has fallen
The last color of the street
Yellow, red
And six months of my life

6 décembre, 1990
New Haven, CT

Le cimetière des mots

Pointu
Penché
Tordu

Bouilloire
Grenouille
Gribouiller

Pou
Ouag
Dg

Salon d'été
Les Rajfra discutent philo
L'ébouillanthé

Mots de passe partout

Inventer de nouveaux mots
Qui ne signifieront rien
Pour toi
Oublier les anciens mots
Les enterrer

Dans le cimetière des mots

16 mars 1991
New Haven, CT

Un manteau court rose (A pink short coat)

Tout d'abord la curiosité
Ça ne devait pas marcher
La honte de lui faire perdre son temps
Des fleurs séchées à l'eau de rose
Dans le papier à lettre
Mais pas le baratin habituel des
« avec les pieds sur terre » et des
« avec sens de l'humour »
Jeune « travaillant dans les études Juives »
Mais ce répondeur
Cette voix aigüe décidée
Volontaire professionnelle impersonnelle

Un brunch
Qui ne devait pas durer
Qui n'était pas fait pour durer
Des boucles d'oreilles
Des cheveux courts bouclés blonds
Des boucles d'oreilles
En forme de colimaçon
Un foulard serré autour du cou
Noué strictement
Un brunch qui ne pouvait pas durer

Un brunch
Une promenade à travers le Village
Dans le froid
Un café
Une partie de billard, un vrai billard
Prendre des billets pour le soir
Un café avec trop de lumière
Aider deux handicapes en chaise roulante
A descendre d'un trottoir

Objectivement gentille mais rationnelle

Une boite de jazz
La première séance
Une lumière dans ses yeux
Quand elle m'a cru éduqué
La vue de son cou nu
Quand son foulard s'est défait
Le foulard renoué consciencieusement

La deuxième séance
Sa façon d'accepter une main
Sa façon d'attendre et d'imiter doucement
Sa façon d'avoir parfois la main humide
Sa façon de se laisser embrasser sur le cou
Au bas du foulard

Et puis le taxi
Le taxi qui a pour chauffeur une femme
Le taxi qui dépasse son appartement
Et qui est obligé de faire un détour
Beni soit le taxi

Une idée bizarre
Dire à ses amis
Se marier à la synagogue avec un Rabbin
Avec un Rabbin
Se marier avec un Rabbin.
Un enfant à l'école
Répondant à une question
« Mon père est psychiatre
Ma mère est Rabbin »

Un Rabbin avec un manteau court rose

New York, le 21 février 1990

Nous reviendrons (We will be back)

« **1** ; 25 ; 14 ; 30 » Le petit livre égrainait les anniversaires de mariage
« 50 ; 60 ; 88 » et les anniversaires de naissances
« Romantique ; Endroit spécial ; Charmant »
Les weekends du Labor Day et du Mémorial Day étaient les plus populaires
« Nous reviendrons, promis » mais pas de nouvelle entrée des mêmes dans le petit livre.

Qu'étaient-ils devenus ? Tous ces couples ayant passé la nuit dans le lit à baldaquin en face de la cheminée, pour donner un coup de jeune à leur relation.

Etaient-ils toujours ensemble, ou séparés par la mort ?
Etaient-ils toujours capable de faire l'amour ?
Etait-elle flétrie par l'âge et lui par les rhumatismes ?

L'endroit paraissait refait à neuf. Pas de télévision. Uniquement des moments précieux à partager avec son conjoint.

Et les couples illégitimes ? Ils n'avaient pas laissé de trace sur le petit livre, marquant leur présence seulement par l'absence d'entrée à certaines années lors des weekends les plus populaires.

« Œufs Benedict, quiche, succulent petit déjeuner, hôtesse attentionnée »
Qui lisait donc ce petit livre ? Qui pensait à y répondre mais ne le faisait pas ?
Qui était surpris de réaliser que cette chambre à coucher n'était pas vraiment la leur, pas seulement pour eux ?

Qui répondait au petit livre ?

La femme, avec une écriture bien ronde et polie, comme on écrit dans son journal intime
Qui s'excusait d'être ici ? Qui ne se sentait pas faisant partie du club
Et parcourait embarrassé les entrées du petit livre ?

Non, ce n'était pas possible.
Avant d'avoir découvert ce journal collectif
L'endroit paraissait le notre
Sans fantôme, sans passé
Flottant dans le temps

Et l'amour
Faire l'amour
Rejouer la nuit de noce
Et la tendresse

Nous reviendrons

Le 22 juin 1995

אינשאללה (Insh'Allah)

18 יוני 2004 (בסוף שנת השבתון)
ירושלים, קטמון הישנה

איך אפשר לעזוב את ירושלים?
איך נפרדים מירושלים?

אי אפשר לעזוב את ירושלים כמו את פריס או את ניו יורק. אין מרגישים אשמה כשעוזבים את ניו יורק או את פריס. "אתה רוצה לעזוב? טוב לך. תיהנה."
ירושלים, היא משהו אחר. מרגישים אחריות כלפי אחרים לחיות פה, אחריות לא רק לתושבי הארץ, אבל גם למי שהפך אותנו לשליחים משותפים ב-"חלום הירושלמי".

איך עוזבים את ירושלים, המרכז של העולם היהודי, שלקראתה מכוונים את לבבינו ואת בתי הכנסת שלנו?
לאמיתו של דבר, אי אפשר. יותר מניו יורק או פריס, חוזרים עם חלק של ירושלים עמנו.

עם איזה חלק מירושלים אני אחזור?
בוודאות אבי, הבן הבכור שלנו, יליד הארץ; וגם את בנותנו שמדברות עברית עכשיו; וכמובן סוזן אישתי. היא תהיה כמו ירושלים הפרטית שלי, עם זיכרונותינו המשותפים.

ירושלים הפרטית שלנו תשתתף עם חלקים אחרים של ירושלים שמצאנו בניו יורק ושעוד חסרים בישראל,
כמו הקהילה הקדושה שלנו של "אור זרוע", הרב שלנו, ועמיתינו שעושים עבודת קודש במרפאה בבורו פארק.

אנחנו נזכור לא רק את ירושלים של מעלה
אבל גם את ירושלים של מטה,
עם ציפוריה שמתעוררות ומזמרות כמו עכשיו בחמש בבוקר,
עם פריחה, עם כוכביה בשמים,
עם האוויר הורוד בערב והחום היבש באמצע היום,
עם שכנינו הנחמדים והנהגים התוקפניים.
עם המורות המתמסרות, אסתי וחגית,
שגרמו חוויה משמעותית לילדותינו בירושלים,
עם חבריהן מבית הספר ומהגן, עם חברינו מהאולפן,

עם מישל בן דודי,
עם החתולים ברחובות,
עם נמל התעופה,
ועם המטוס.

ואם ירצה השם, נשוב אליך ירושלים,
גוד ווילינג[28], אינשאללה, סי דיע וע[29].

דניאל רוזן
ניו יורק, 24 נובמבר 2005

---

[28] God willing (איה"ש = אם ירצה השם, באנגלית)
[29] Si Dieu veut (איה"ש בצרפתית)

8 Just a brunch
A Psychiatrist's Narrative

The question 189-190
The sacrifice of Sarah 191-193
I swear! I swear! I swear! 194
The sacrifice of Tamás 195-201
The list 202-205
The brunch 206

"Maybe it was time for him to bury his own."
Page 38

The question

But why is it important for you that I come to brunch on Sunday?
Just like that, I would like you to come.

She was right. Why was it so important? It was just a brunch. Me and her younger brother, Avi, my new friend and her children: her daughter and her son, Sammy. Avi had not met any of them and Sammy was about to leave in two days just after the last holiday of this season. It was the last opportunity for them to meet, before Sammy returned to the army. The two sons, hers and mine, Avi 14 and Sammy 20. They may click.

It would be nice if they could just meet. Not just nice. Important. Sammy could be a role model for Avi, and Sammy could talk to him about being a combat medic in the engineering forces. Avi for sure would be interested, he who spends so much time on video games gunning invisible enemies. Maybe it would entice Avi to join the army when he finishes high school, like it is required from everyone who lives in the country.

Oh no, my grandmother, Sarah, lost a son in the resistance. And I would want him to join the army and risk his life? For what? To be a hero like Tamás, the brother of my father? To repair the loss of a resistance fighter with no army and no country? To make it right this time? To avenge Tamás' death, and give meaning to it?

What is that call to push Avi into that journey? Let the boy be a boy. Let him live as a boy who has friends and plays video games. Did Abraham have that call too, when he led his son

Isaac to be sacrificed? Sarah too had a son called Isaac, and he was also led to be sacrificed. But Tamás saved him and took his place. Avi is just a boy. What does he have to do with that ancient history?

Avi had agreed to the brunch. He said in an uncharacteristic response that he would go if I wanted him to. Maybe I was hoping he would refuse. Don't start down this path.

The sacrifice of Sarah

Don't go too far
The mother implored
Her son, her precious, her unique
Her soul bound to his
Her son
She bore at ninety years

The bound one, the fragrance, and the tears.

I see the fire, the wood and the devouring knife
But where is the sacrifice?
The son wondered
God will choose the sacrifice,:
My son

The bound one, the fragrance, and the tears.

The son went up the mountain
To the altar
Bound like a ram
An offering of pleasant fragrance
To be accepted in favor before God

The bound one, the fragrance, and the tears.

The knife above his neck
The tears running along his cheeks
The eyes blurred
The heart racing

The bound one, the fragrance, and the tears.

Tell my mother
That her joy has passed
Her son was food to the devouring knife.
Who will console you, mother?
Your lament is my pain
Your soul bound to mine.

The bound one, the fragrance, and the tears.

When my flesh is burned
Take the remnants of my ashes
And say to mother:
This is the fragrance of your son.

The bound one, the fragrance, and the tears.

The tears of the angels of the Divine Chariot
Aroused the crying sounds of the shofar
Down to the mother's ears.
She saw from afar
Her son to be sacrificed.
She joined the tears of the shofar
And her soul departed.

The bound one, the fragrance, and the tears.

I should have been there
Lamented the mother.
I'm a mother, I have good instincts
I would have shouted to him
Be careful of that rock
There are explosives there!
I don't know anything about the army
But I do know how to be a mother.

The bound one, the fragrance, and the tears.

In his pants pockets I found
Drawings his children made for him
Along with a book of Tehilim
He had taken with him on the mission.

The bound one, the fragrance and the tears.

When they brought me his tallit
I sniffed it
It smelled of the army
Of the grease they use on rifles.

The bound one, the fragrance, and the tears.

September 9, 2018; Erev Rosh Hashana 5779
Homage to "Et Shaarei Ratson"[30]. Thanks to Miriam Peretz[31]

---

[30] https://www.jardindelatorah.org/shaare-ratson-rosh-hashana-orel-gozlan/
[31] Shir, Smadar. *The Story of Miriam Peretz: Miriam's Song*, p.313-314. Gefen Publishing House, Jerusalem, 2016. Quoted by Michal Horowitz. *Putting Our Hearts Back Into Our Prayers*, Rosh Hashana To-Go 5779. https://www.yutorah.org/togo/roshhashana/

I swear! I swear! I swear!

When Avi learned about Tamás' heroic action in the war, he told his older sister that it meant he would have to save her life like Tamás. And he would. Avi is the kind of guy you want to have in your foxhole. I witnessed that selflessness when he played basketball. When he scored a goal, he did not even check if the ball went into the basket. He continued, focused on helping his team to continue fighting the game. He could have at least enjoyed, for one second the goal he made, an achievement worth savoring and worth the recognition of his peers and the parents. When the game was over, he said that he did not have time to check. Clearly, it was not about him scoring, it was about his team winning. I would trust this guy with my life in a combat situation. "Never leave a wounded man in the field. This I swear! I swear! I swear!" shouted Sammy in unison with all his comrades at the graduation ceremony from his training as a combat medic. Avi would fit right in.

Telling the story of Tamás is more like passing a testimony, a testament, a will, a model. Be careful.

The sacrifice of Tamás

"You think I don't know?"
Sarah went out of the cab where her son Isaac had left her, pretending to go into the building for no important reason.
"You don't think I know?"
Sarah put her scarf around her head, covering her hair and tying it up with a small knot under her chin; the same scarf she would use when lighting the Sabbath candles. She followed her son and his wife along with her grandson who was still a little boy. They went to the back of the synagogue, on the western wall, toward the memorial plaques. There was a mention of Tamás who died during the Shoah in Budapest as a resistance fighter. His comrades in his underground Zionist movement must have put that plaque in his memory after the war when they immigrated to the Promised Land. How did Sarah and Isaac learn separately about that synagogue? The story does not tell. Now, approximately 50 years after that visit to Tamás' memorial plaque around 1971, the placement of this synagogue near Tel Aviv (possibly in Petach Tikva) has been forgotten, and it is unclear if the synagogue is still standing. The names of Tamás' comrades who kept him in their memory were also forgotten. Only the story persists. And the story shall still have the same power as being by the plaque.

Issac had wanted to spare his mother who could not accept having lost a son at the end of 1944. After the war, they had all requested immigrant visas to go to the United States: In the visa application, David and Sarah/Margit ("Marguerite") had listed their two sons with their already Americanized first name, Isaac/Endre/André ("Andrew") and Tamás/Mordechai Zvi ("Thomas"). They included their dead son, because who knows, he may still show up, or maybe to appease Sarah's pain. The silence about Tamás between Sarah and her older surviving son, Isaac, persisted even to the day of the visit of Tamás' plaque, about 25 years after the end of the Shoah. However on May 16, 1955, David had come to Yad Vashem and submitted a testimony page for Tamás Rajna. Did he inform his wife? We will never know. All we can see are a few words written in Hebrew on the form: Circumstance of death: "disappeared". An alias was also noted in that testimony page: Horváth (Károly) Kálmán.[32] On that day David wrote a total of 10 testimony pages including pages for his mother and 4 sisters and other close relatives[33]. A minyan of dead victims. May their memory be a blessing.

David and Sarah did not immigrate to the United States, and their son did not use his Americanized first name. Instead, they settled in Tel Aviv in 1949. Sarah was a very fervent Zionist and kept saying to her grandson after the war, that Israel was the place for Jews. André reported that his mother did not look Jewish during the war, and therefore could get out of the apartment where her husband David was hidden outside the Budapest Ghetto. She fabricated false papers for the Jewish underground, and she may have written a false identity card for her son Tamás. That false paper survived the

---

[32] https://yvng.yadvashem.org/nameDetails.html?language=en&itemId=1438013&ind=5
[33] David reported that his 91 year old mother, Malka Risze, died in Auschwitz. Also were killed 4 sisters (Rózsi, Pepi, Etel, and Sára), one nephew (Avraham David, son of his sister Sára), along with the siblings of his wife Sarah: two sisters (Elza and Kornélia) and Sándor, her brother.
https://yvng.yadvashem.org/nameDetails.html?language=en&itemId=3895491&ind=0
https://yvng.yadvashem.org/nameDetails.html?language=en&itemId=1098883&ind=0
https://yvng.yadvashem.org/nameDetails.html?language=en&itemId=931419&ind=2
https://yvng.yadvashem.org/nameDetails.html?language=en&itemId=382776&ind=1
https://yvng.yadvashem.org/nameDetails.html?language=en&itemId=1421271&ind=2
https://yvng.yadvashem.org/nameDetails.html?language=en&itemId=1438454&ind=3
https://yvng.yadvashem.org/nameDetails.html?language=en&itemId=355719&ind=3
https://yvng.yadvashem.org/nameDetails.html?language=en&itemId=315697&ind=4
https://yvng.yadvashem.org/nameDetails.html?language=en&itemId=1501960&ind=0

war. André explained that with a false certificate, as Christian (and two years older), Tamás was able to request an official Hungarian driver's license. Like his mother, Tamás did not look Jewish. He also appeared older than his age. At the age of 17, he had to undertake the physical examination required in order to get his driver's license.

Tamás could have stayed in hiding in the relative comfort of his parent's apartment. And nobody would have criticized a 17 year old boy who chose to do so. Instead, he went to the physical examination. We could imagine him in his white underwear in a line like the others waiting their turn. André told his son that during that visit during the war in a Hungary cooperating with the Germans, Tamás went so sure of himself, looking confident (André mimicked a straight posture), that the examiner did not bother pulling down his underwear to check, as required, if he was circumcised. Would his circumcision have been discovered, his false papers under a Christian identity would have been of no use to him, and he would have been immediately arrested and deported.

With that driver's license, tells André, Tamás got a job as a driver at the German Embassy in Budapest. For that job, he wore an armband with the swastika. He used his position to transmit fake orders of transferring Jews away from labor camp. This is how he transferred his older brother André from a forced labor camp in Hungary (a mine near the town of Tata, in the Balkony Mountains, according to André's report) to a transit camp inside Budapest. The prisoners in those labor camps mostly perished, for example by being killed on the spot by their guards, or by being sent to slaughter to the Russian front, or to "death marches" and concentration camps[34]. From the transit camp, André was able to escape when he volunteered for unloading heavy bags of coal to the residence of a German official in Budapest. By the third day, he had gained some trust from the armed guard who was watching them, and André, who did not even smoke, asked if he could buy a pack of cigarettes from the store around the corner. It happened that this corner store had two entries. André walked in one door, turned and walked out the other, and rejoined his parents in hiding at their apartment outside the ghetto of Budapest.

Folded with Tamás' fake Christian identity card, was a surprising paper: A membership card to the Hungarian Youth League, a voluntary Hungarian military organization affiliated with the Arrow Cross, a Nazi inspired anti-Semite far-right party who was placed in power in Hungary by the Germans starting October 1944. That paper certifies that Tamás Stibinger is a member of that League who is expected to show up to the barracks on December 16, 1944. Was this another fake paper, or did Tamás really joined that fascist organization? Tamás had already been working at the German Embassy in Budapest, so volunteering for an Arrow Cross organization could not have been more dangerous.

Tamás did not survive the war. According to the report of one of the prisoners to the family, he was discovered and shot. There was never any formal proof of his death. He just disappeared. And his mother Sarah waited for many long years hoping that maybe her son would come back, one day.

---

[34] See: https://www.ushmm.org/research/scholarly-presentations/conferences/the-holocaust-in-hungary-70-years-later/the-holocaust-in-hungary-frequently-asked-questions#6

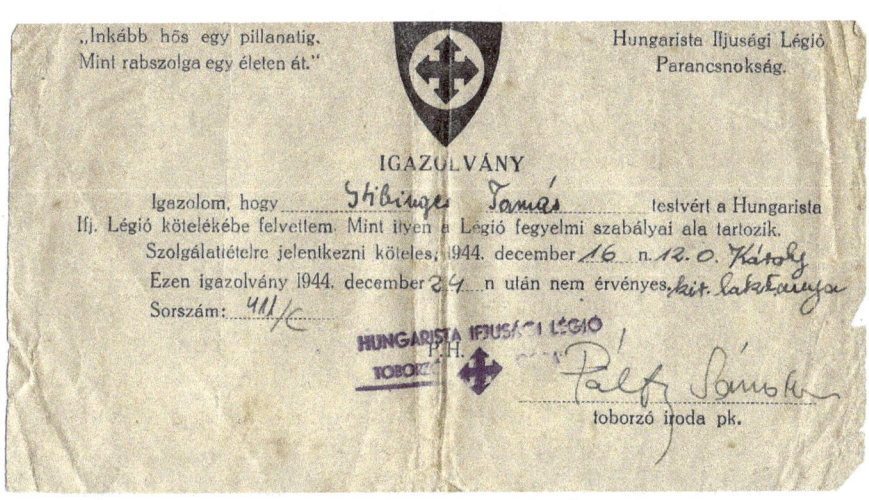

Tamás' membership card to a Nazi inspirited military organization.

From: 117-9-4@auswaertiges-amt.de
Sent: Wednesday, February 23, 2005 5:29 AM
Subject: your request concerning your uncle Tamas Rajna

Auswärtiges Amt
Politisches Archiv
Gz.: 117-251.09 R
(bei Antwort bitte angeben)

Dear Mr. Rajna,

The German embassy in Budapest has forwarded your request to the archives of the Ministry of Foreign Affairs. Unfortunately there is practically no archival material of the former German legation in Budapest left, as far as matters of the local legation-staff in the last years before 1945 is concerned. The only data-base I have is the pay-role duplicates which the legation sent to the ministry in Berlin. On these, however, I could not find your uncle with either of his names. Neither could I find any report on his death.
I regret very much this unsatisfactory result.
Sincerely
pp

Dr. Gerhard Keiper

The unsatisfactory result when searching the pay-role duplicates from the former German legation in Budapest could be explained if Tamás used a different false name, or if he was an independent contractor not on the legation's payroll. The oral testimony of André to his son is consistent with the written report of his father to Yad Vashem. It also fits with the false Christian identity card under the name of Kovács Kálmán still in the family's possession. The memory of that plaque in that synagogue was also consistent with André's testimony. Time has passed and Tamás' comrades are not here anymore to corroborate André's testimony. But the 10 pages written by David are still here, as a memorial. Traditionally, 10 living men gather to recite the Mourner's *Kaddish*, the prayer for the dead, in order to remember a departed relative. The *Kaddish* does not mention death and is only a praise to God, "may His name be adorned exalted and worshiped". It is expected to be of great merit for the soul of the deceased, to have a living relative recite that prayer.[35] But here, on that day of 1955, as soon as the tenth name of those holy martyrs was entered, it is they who all started reciting the prayer of the dead, the *Kaddish*, for their surviving relative who remembered them, David, in order to help him and his family survive difficult times, thanks to the merit of their ancestors.

---

[35] See for example:
https://www.chabad.org/library/article_cdo/aid/255986/jewish/Why-Do-Mourners-Recite-Kaddish.htm

Tamás' fake identity card (front and back), under the name of "E. Kovács Kálmán" (Kovács being the last name), son of Ilona Szabó, born on June 23, 1925.

The religion (box number 4) is described as "r.k.", an abbreviation for "római katolikus" (Roman Catholic).

The occupation (box number 6) is described as "ker. isk. tanuló", an abbreviation for "keresztény iskola tanuló", meaning "Christian school student."

The list

New York, September 20. 2004

Dear Maurice, Dear Amira,

Barukh Dayan Haemet (Blessed be the Just Judge). Nobody died recently in my family, however I feel that it is overwhelming to just learn of their loss now; and I feel like saying the Hebrew formula when you hear such awful news.
I was just looking at a newspaper online when I clicked on an advertisement from Yad Vashem. In no time, I found the 1955 testimony of my grandfather about his son (my uncle) Tamas (Mordekhai Tzvi) Rajna. I knew this testimony already, since right after I mentioned Tamás to Yad Vashem on September 2001, they mailed me a hard copy of that testimony, well before the opening of their web database. That had been emotional enough, since the only writing and signature I have from my late grandfather is this testimonial page. I just clicked on the "Related Searches: Pages of Testimony by the same submitter" and I got the awful news: my grand-father had left testimonies for his mother (Malka), his sister (Miriam), his sister in law (Elisheva Ester), and his nephew (Avraham David). (We have named our 1 year old son David Avraham!) Nobody else filed a testimony about their death. Who will remember them?

Dan

Dearest Friends. Unfortunately there is more. I was curious, and I typed "Rosenheck" (my grandfather's name before he changed it to "Rajna") and I found more testimonies from him: His sister Sara, and two other sisters-in-law. All those testimonies were made the same day on May 16th, 1955. How many testimonies did he submit that day? I feel like I opened a bottomless pit. I looked at your last name, Maurice (with only one T): there are 76 names. God bless their souls.

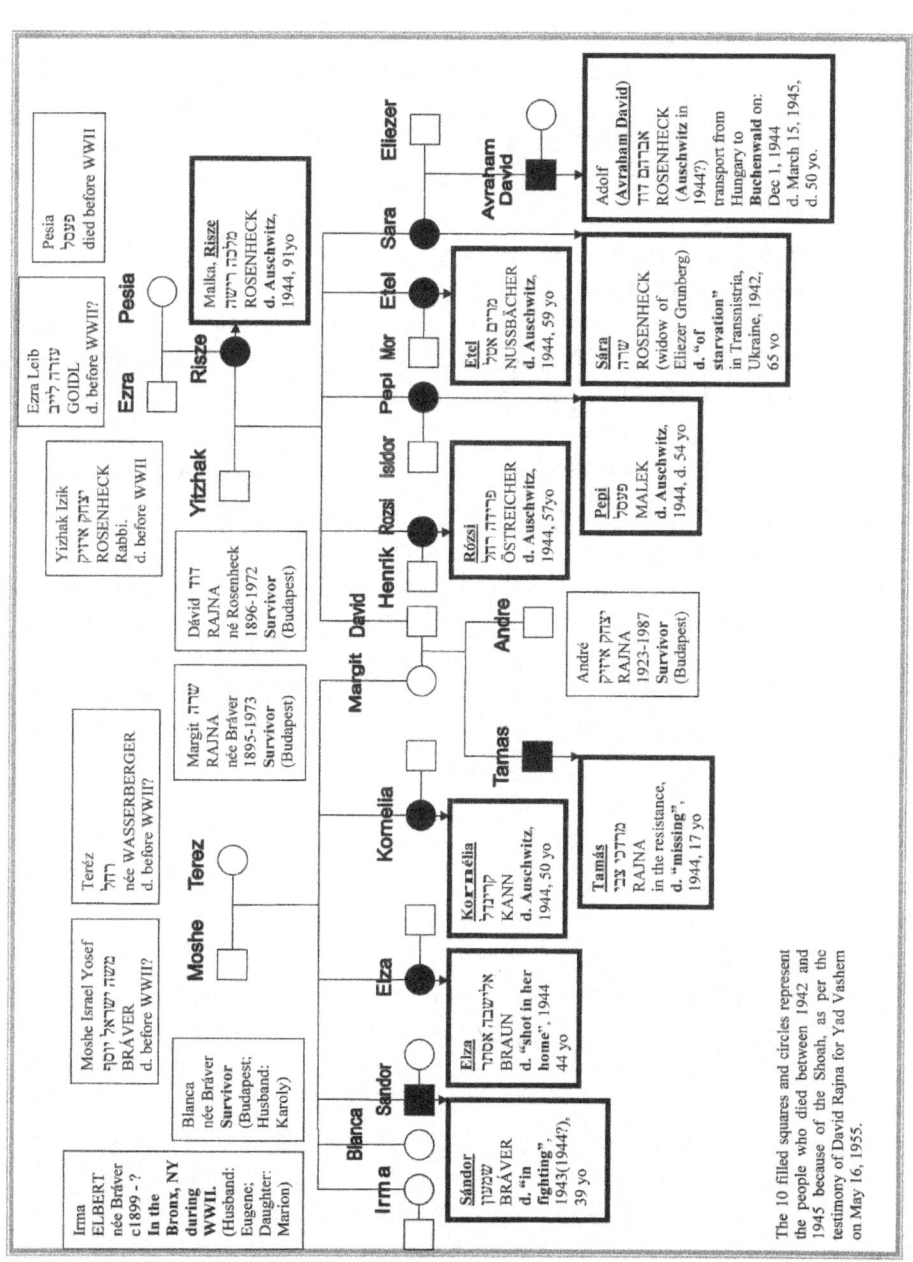

The 10 filled squares and circles represent the people who died between 1942 and 1945 because of the Shoah, as per the testimony of Dávid Rajna for Yad Vashem on May 16, 1955.

Tamás (Mordechai Zvi) Rajna — "disappeared"
Age 17; Dec 29, 1944
Son of David & Margit (Sarah) Rajna.

Malka Risze (Malka Risha) Rosenheck — Auschwitz
Age 91; 1944; mother of David Rajna.

Rózsi (Frida Rachel) Östreicher — Auschwitz
Age 57; 1944; sister of David Rajna.

Pepi (Pesel) Malek — Auschwitz
Age 54; 1944; sister of David Rajna.

Etel (Miriam Etel) Nussbächer — Auschwitz
Age 59; 1944; sister of David Rajna.

Sára (Sarah) Rosenheck — died "of starvation"
Age 65; 1942; sister of David Rajna.

Adolf (Avraham David) Rosenheck — Auschwitz
Age 50, 1944; son of Sára Rosenheck

Sándor (Shimon) Bráver — died "in fighting"
Age 39; February 14, 1943
Brother of Margit (Sarah) Rajna.

Elza (Elisheva Esther) Braun — "shot in her home"
Age 44; October 15, 1944;
Sister of Margit (Sarah) Rajna.

Kornélia (Krindel) Kann — Auschwitz
Age 50; 1944;
Sister of Margit (Sarah) Rajna.

The list in Hebrew:

"נעלם"	מרדכי צבי בן דוד ושָׂרָה
אושוויץ	מלכה רישה בת עזרה לייב ופעסל
אושוויץ	פרידה רחל בת יצחק איזיק ומלכה רישה
אושוויץ	פעסל בת יצחק איזיק ומלכה רישה
אושוויץ	מרים אטל בת יצחק איזיק ומלכה רישה
"מרעב"	שרה בת יצחק איזיק ומלכה רישה
אושוויץ	אברהם דוד בן שרה ואליעזר
"בקרב"	שמעון בן משה ישראל יוסף ורחל
"נורתה בביתה"	אלישבה אסתר בת משה ישראל יוסף ורחל
אושוויץ	קרינדל בת משה ישראל יוסף ורחל

This is part of the Yad Vashem testimony where David mentions Tamás' aliases and his correct date of birth, September 6, 1927. The testimony of David and André related to Tamás and the 9 other victims is a true story. Tamás ID and membership cards are true copies from the wartime family archives.

The brunch

The brunch? It did not happen. Everybody was busy on the eve of the final holiday. And Sammy's mind was into the preparation of returning to Israel for his final week of exercise in the army: A rite de passage where he would be in the field for an entire week, in full battle gear, culminating with a 60 km march with his bag and army equipment. Avi's mind was also somewhere else, preparing for an exam to get into a better high school of his choice.

Only the unknown future would have told us if this skipped brunch was a missed opportunity, or a close call.

New York, October 3, 2018

9 The oldnew bracelet
Relationship with the ancestors

Le nouveau-vieux bracelet (*in French*) 209-226
The platter   227-232
The bracelet   233-243
Nouna   245-255
Forever ephemeral   257
The scrum (La mêlée)   259-263

Le nouveau-vieux bracelet

This chapter is the French translation by the author of the next three chapters.
Ce chapitre est la traduction par l'auteur des 3 prochains chapitres.
L'original en Anglais inclus des photos et une table généalogique.

Le plateau

Non, dit Élise. Je veux le mien, pas celui-ci. Huguette ne comprenait pas pourquoi elle était si têtue. Huguette, sa belle-sœur, lui avait déniché un plateau en cuivre semblable à celui que Zahri, la mère d'Élise, avait préparé pour son mariage: trois plateaux en cuivre, un pour chacune de ses trois filles. Les deux aînées, Fernande et Yvonne, avaient reçu leur cadeau de mariage. Malheureusement, Zahri était décédée avant le mariage d'Élise et n'avait jamais eu la chance de lui donner le sien. Lison, comme on appelait Élise, avait perdu son plateau en cuivre. C'était une injustice qui n'avait aucune valeur monétaire. C'était un lien avec une mère bien-aimée, le souvenir de l'amour d'une mère, une mère qui était partie beaucoup trop tôt. Une mère dont la photo en noir et blanc avait toujours été sur le piano dans leur modeste appartement parisien toutes ces années, jusqu'à ce qu'Élise déménage plus tard dans un appartement plus grand, avec le même piano et la même photo, jusqu'à ce qu'elle déménage encore dans la chambre d'une maison sans son piano, mais toujours avec la même photo, jusqu'à ce qu'elle se demande d'où elle, Élise, venait.

Malgré tout, Lison avait un objet qui lui rappelait sa mère. Elle avait son bracelet en or. Un bracelet qu'elle porterait tout le temps. Un simple mais beau bracelet avec une rangée de petites pyramides carrées faisant saillie vers l'extérieur et entourant le poignet. Un motif étrange, à la fois ancien et moderne, reliant des générations de femmes. Sa mère ou sa grand-mère portait plusieurs bracelets à la fois, et chaque fille avait pu en avoir un. Lison y était particulièrement attaché. Son initiale y était gravée, un L fleuri, interrompant le cercle des pyramides, adaptation moderne d'un bijou ancien. Zahri avait dû l'obtenir de sa propre mère, Esther, probablement comme cadeau de mariage, pour sa dot. Il aurait très certainement accompagné un plateau en cuivre, perpétuant la chaîne des mères, des ancêtres aux filles, une transmission matrilinéaire du patrimoine culturel génétique complémentant leur ADN mitochondrial.

Qui possédait le plateau en cuivre d'Élise ? Micheline, sa belle-sœur, l'avait pris après son mariage, la même année mais avant celui d'Élise. Jusque-là, le plateau était resté bien sagement dans son coin, attendant le mariage d'Élise, la troisième sœur. Élise n'a pas dû être là pour le réclamer. Et puis le mari de Micheline était également décédé, et Micheline avait conservé l'héritage, l'affichant fièrement pendant au moins 30 ans chez elle, et n'avait pas voulu restituer ce souvenir qui maintenant lui était propre. Pour elle, le plateau en cuivre convoité par Élise était un récit concurrent, une lutte pour le passé qui affectait le présent. Et puis Micheline était elle-même décédée, et qui sait parmi ses enfants celui qui a hérité du plateau en cuivre de Lison. Lison n'est plus de ce monde pour le réclamer. Mais la chaîne, la chaîne, la chaîne des mères tient toujours, tant que leurs souvenirs sont vivants et que les petites-filles d'Élise, Leah Zahri (nommée après la mère d'Élise) et Miriam, sont prêtes à transmettre leur héritage.[36]

Trois plateaux. Trois filles. Fernande, Yvonne et Élise. Y avait-il un message secret qui ne pouvait être découvert que si les trois plateaux étaient réunis, comme les trois parchemins appartenant aux trois frères dans *Le secret de la Licorne* de

---

[36] Les prénoms des petites filles d'Élise ont été changés pour ce récit.

Tintin ? Zahri et ses aïeules espéraient-elles que la tradition serait poursuivie et qu'on se souviendrait d'elles ? Est-ce que Zahri, Élise et toutes les femmes avant elles tentaient de se lier avec Leah Zahri et Miriam ?

Les trois filles avaient déjà rejoint leur mère, Zahri, dans le monde à venir, enfin réunies. La fille aînée de Fernande aurait hérité du plateau en cuivre. Il a été transmis à sa famille et pourrait être retrouvé. Yvonne, la deuxième fille de Zahri, vivait à Toulon dans le sud de la France à la fin de sa vie et elle exhibait aussi fièrement son plateau. Il était accroché au mur, au-dessus du canapé de son charmant petit appartement toujours d'une propreté éclatante, avec une terrasse et une vue sur la mer Méditerranée. Yvonne aimait bien parler. Elle était la seule à pouvoir réduire au silence sa sœur cadette, Lison. Yvonne appliquait le Midrash à sa mère Zahri, expliquant comment le prophète Élie bénissait une maison accueillante et décrivant comment la maison de Zahri était ouverte aux invités.

Yvonne et Lison ont raconté la même histoire de la préparation d'une table de fête pour les nombreux membres de la famille (les 3 sœurs avaient également 5 frères), avec très peu d'espace entre les sièges. Néanmoins, Zahri exigeait d'ajouter un siège supplémentaire. « Mais pourquoi ?» a demandé Yvonne à sa mère. « J'ai bien compté. Nous n'avons pas besoin d'un siège en plus. » Yvonne se rappelait avec fierté ce que sa mère avait répondu: « Si quelqu'un vient à l'improviste et ne voit pas un siège vide, il pourrait penser qu'il n'est pas le bienvenu. »

Yvonne se souvenait également de la réponse de sa mère lorsque des membres pauvres de la famille venaient et volaient le peu argent qui se trouvait dans l'entrée. Yvonne avait alerté sa mère de ce petit vol. Zahri répondit: « Je sais qu'ils me volent, ma fille. Je laisse l'argent là exprès. Parfois, c'est difficile de demander. »

Le plateau en cuivre d'Yvonne n'était plus sur son mur. Il était placé au-dessus d'une étagère dans le salon de sa fille Danielle. La mémoire de ce plateau est toujours là et sa photo montre un plateau en cuivre ciselé avec un motif rare et original. Le lien avec le passé n'est pas rompu. D'autres traditions et histoires ont survécu, du moins en mémoire:

Le verre d'eau qu'une mère vide sur le sol devant la porte en direction d'un membre de la famille sur le point de partir, pour lui souhaiter bonne chance et pour qu'il revienne en bonne santé, en disant en arabe « *trek slemme* », « va en paix. »[37]

Le plateau du *seder* tourné trois fois au-dessus de la tête de chaque participant au début de la lecture de la *hagadah*, l'histoire de Pâque.

La pièce de monnaie en or (*Louis d'or*) posée sur le couscous au beurre pour la Mimouna, la fête marquant la fin de la Pâque.

Le souvenir affectueux du « four banal », four communautaire où les familles juives apportaient leur nourriture le vendredi après-midi, afin de prendre un repas chaud le jour du Chabat et contourner ainsi l'interdiction de la cuisson.

Le soupir accompagné des mots arabes « *Aye imeh !*» (Signifiant « Oh mère !»), quand tout n'allait pas si bien.

La préparation de dernière minute par les femmes, du repas pour le couper le jeûne de Yom Kippour lorsqu'elles entendaient les hommes chanter *besha'at haneïla* dans la synagogue voisine avec une ardeur renouvelée pour l'office final.

Le partage sans fin des petits gâteaux de fête faits maison avec leur saveur traditionnelle, unissant tous les proches comme une chaîne de lettres, de la femme qui les a préparés au reste de la famille, rejoignant même ses membres vivant au loin; chacun devant faire passer un morceau de

---

[37] Voir: https://azititou.wordpress.com/2012/06/29/le-verre-deau/

mémoire savoureux à un enfant, un frère, une sœur, un être cher, pour transmettre la tradition, la connexion au passé, aux ancêtres, au vieux pays, jusqu'aux dernières miettes.

Et bien sûr, il y avait le bracelet. Le bracelet en or de Lison orné d'un « $\mathscr{L}$ » fleuri.

Le bracelet

Écrire l'histoire pour que l'histoire ne se répète pas. Écrire l'histoire du bracelet pour que l'histoire du plateau en cuivre ne se répète pas, afin que le bracelet aille à qui il est destiné, perpétuant ainsi la chaîne de relations entre générations, entre les vivants et les morts, entre les ancêtres et leurs descendants, entre les mères et les filles, et les filles qui sont elles-mêmes devenues mères.

Un bracelet en or. Deux filles. Un bracelet manquant. La mère de Zahri portait de nombreux bracelets, selon la coutume, et leur nombre diminuait de génération en génération. Le bracelet en or de Lison, déjà marqué d'un L, ira à sa petite-fille la plus âgée, Leah, le jour de son mariage, si Dieu veut. Miriam aura un nouveau bracelet. Un nouveau-vieux bracelet, un nouveau bracelet fait avec de l'ancien, comme le nouveau-vieux pays, Israël, l'Altneuland de Theodore Herzl ou l'ancienne nouvelle synagogue de Prague, l'Altneuschul.

Mais où trouver un nouveau bracelet comme l'ancien ?

Miriam et son père ne pouvaient plus aller en Algérie pour des raisons de sécurité. Toutefois, Sidi-Bel-Abbès et Oran sont proches du Maroc. Les coutumes juives de l'ouest algérien sont similaires à celles du Maroc voisin, et certains des ancêtres étaient clairement originaires de ce pays. La réponse était dans l'immense souk de Marrakech. Niché au milieu des senteurs et des couleurs du souk des épices, du souk des tapis, du souk des forgerons, du souk des babouches, du souk des potiers, et du souk des teinturiers, se trouvait un magasin avec une étonnante trouvaille: un antique bracelet en argent, brillant, et ressemblant à celui en or. Le vendeur expliqua que les pyramides du bracelet avaient à l'origine une fonction utilitaire, outre sa qualité esthétique: il était utilisé par les laveuses pour frotter un point sale en essayant de le nettoyer. Et, ajouta le vendeur, c'était un bijou berbère.

Un bijou berbère ? Élise était-elle une descendante par sa mère d'une tribu berbère convertie au judaïsme avant l'arrivée de l'islam au Maghreb ?

Miriam était tellement heureuse d'avoir son nouveau bracelet, notamment à cause de la nouvelle connexion avec un passé qu'elle était en train de construire. Même si la chaîne ininterrompue de femmes avait sauté une génération en passant par son père. Ici, dans un petit magasin du souk de Marrakech, elle a trouvé des réponses sur l'origine de sa grand-mère, sur sa propre origine. Au retour de ce voyage au Maroc, quand elle a entendu parler de la provenance berbère du bijou de famille, Danielle a rapporté que sa mère, Yvonne, la sœur d'Élise, soupçonnait également avoir des racines berbères, à cause des chansons berbères que Zahri lui chantait quand Yvonne était enfant.

Et puis il y avait trois noms berbères dans la famille d'Élise. Cachés en pleine vue. Aknin et Laïk du côté maternel, et Draï du côté paternel.[1]

Aknin est un diminutif du nom Akan en langue berbère, et il signifie « petit Jacob ».

Draï est un nom associé à une tribu juive berbère de l'oued Draa, un fleuve du sud du Maroc. La tradition orale familiale rapportée par Prosper, affirme qu'au moins une branche de sa famille venait de Tafilalet. Tafilalet est situé dans cette même région marocaine appelée Drâa-Tafilalet. « Pourquoi es-tu intéressée par ces vieilleries ? » avait répondu Prosper quand Fabienne, sa belle-fille, lui avait posé des questions à propos de ses ancêtres. D'un air de dire que c'était une époque révolue dont on n'était pas spécialement fier, et qu'il était temps de tourner la page : nous sommes civilisés maintenant ! La grand-mère de Fabienne, fière de ses origines de Juive espagnole, parlait encore un espagnol du XVème siècle, à Tétouan. Quand Fabienne lui a annoncé qu'elle voulait se marier avec un jeune homme issu d'une famille juive parlant l'arabe, sa grand-mère lui avait répondu avec dédain : « *Quien habla moro es moro.* » (Celui qui parle arabe est Arabe.[2]) Mais quand Fabienne mentionna la famille de Prosper, sa grand-mère donna son assentiment au mariage : « Avec eux, on peut. Eux, au-moins ils sont civilisés. » Apparemment, à Tétouan, le statut social des Juifs d'origine berbère était bien moins élevé que celui des Juifs d'origine espagnole; mais Prosper avait réussi à estomper le passé berbère de sa famille. Au point où Élise n'avait jamais parlé de Tafilalet et de ses origines tribales, et elle n'en savait probablement rien. Sans les questions de Fabienne, le souvenir de Prosper à propos de Tafilalet aurait été perdu, et seul le nom de Draï aurait survécu.

Le troisième nom, Laïk, le nom de jeune fille de Zahri, est dérivé de *El Haïk*, un nom de famille berbère.[3] Elhaïk est un nom très clairement identifiable comme étant de l'arabe et donc associé à une terre d'islam. Le nom a été transformé, littéralement en le laïcisant, en le rendant plus laïc, tout en gardant une connexion avec le passé et avec la structure de son ancien nom et sa terminaison en « k ». Ce changement de nom exemplifie un processus de sécularisation qui maintient tout de même un lien avec le passé.

Le mot *El Haïk* représente un vêtement berbère (hâyk هايك) d'origine romaine: c'est un long tissu de 1,5 mètre qui est enroulé et maintenu à la taille par une ceinture, puis ramassé sur les épaules où il est maintenu par un crochet; par extension, il correspond en arabe au métier de tisserand.[1] Le haïk était aussi porté par les hommes berbères, comme la toge de la Rome antique, et ne couvrait pas nécessairement le visage. Maintenant, le haïk est voie de disparition et est principalement porté par certaines femmes musulmanes qui l'utilisent comme voile islamique, pour se couvrir le visage à la manière d'un *niqab*.

En plus de sa souche berbère, Élise qui parlait français et espagnol couramment avait, du côté paternel, des noms de famille (Amselem et Sayag) venant de Juifs expulsés d'Espagne en 1492. Ces noms figurent sur une liste publiée les reconnaissant comme éligibles à la procédure accélérée de citoyenneté espagnole en tant que descendants de Juifs expulsés d'Espagne.[4]

Élise s'est battue pour les droits des femmes et méprisait la pratique du voile islamique couvrant leur visage, parce qu'elle le considérait comme oppressif. Quelle ironie qu'Élise, championne de la laïcité, avait une mère dont le nom originel, Laïk, ne signifiait pas « laïc », mais est maintenant associé à un vêtement voilant la face des femmes !

Élise a suivi le chemin de son frère aîné, Roger, et est devenue dentiste, une réussite rare pour une femme algérienne dans les années 50. Élise voulait être médecin mais elle craignait de ne pas être acceptée en tant que femme. Elle pensait qu'elle serait mieux respectée comme dentiste. Cependant, lorsque sa mère est décédée en 1949, Élise, en tant que fille cadette et célibataire, a dû remplir le rôle de sa mère et s'occuper de la maison, de son père et de ses frères. Après un an à jouer ce rôle, elle s'est rendu compte qu'elle gaspillait son diplôme de dentiste et qu'elle resterait vieille fille si elle continuait dans cette voie. Alors, brisant les traditions, elle a quitté son père à Sidi-Bel-Abbès et a racheté un cabinet dentaire à Oran. Seul Dieu peut imaginer à quel point elle s'est sentie coupable de suivre son propre chemin en tant que femme. Une culpabilité mélangée avec une colère envers l'establishment religieux masculin. Encore en rupture avec les traditions, elle a répondu à une annonce matrimoniale (ou peut-être même en a-t-elle placée une, nous ne le saurons jamais) et a épousé un homme juif vivant dans la métropole, comme on appelait autrefois la France métropolitaine, et qui n'était même pas du Maghreb! Élise a gardé toute sa vie le secret de cette annonce matrimoniale. Lorsqu'on lui demandait comment elle avait rencontré son mari de l'autre côté de la mer Méditerranée, elle répondait en souriant la même phrase cryptique: c'était son « jardin secret ».

Même quand sa mémoire s'est estompée, Élise a continué d'être fière, à juste titre, d'être dentiste. Elle a retiré une grande satisfaction de son cabinet dentaire à Paris, même si cela impliquait de longues heures de travail. Élise aimait soigner les travailleurs arabes d'Afrique du Nord, et les Noirs des anciennes colonies françaises d'Afrique. C'étaient ses principaux clients et ils préféraient venir la voir plutôt que d'aller au dispensaire dentaire de la Sécurité Sociale qui était juste à proximité. Ils devaient ressentir une sensibilité commune, au-delà des mots, comme chez eux. Avant de rentrer au pays, ils insistaient pour qu'elle finisse le plus de travaux dentaire possibles, car elle portait le prestige de la métropole. Ses clients voulaient montrer à leur retour qu'ils avaient réussi en France; et leurs sourires ornés d'une dent en or en seraient une preuve visible pour tous. Un client lui a même demandé une fois de lui enlever une dent de devant, une incisive bien saine, pour la remplacer avec une dent en or, ce qu'Élise a refusé.

Malgré sa naissance en Algérie, sa peau était claire, peut-être à cause de ses origines espagnoles. Son nom de femme mariée ne sonnait ni nord-africain, ni juif, et Élise pouvait donc prétendre venir de la France profonde. Elle ne voulait pas révéler qu'elle était « de là-bas » (c'est-à-dire venant d'Algérie) parce qu'elle avait appris qu'il valait mieux ne pas afficher sa judéité.

Élise, femme résolument moderne et émancipée, n'avait pas perdu ses racines ancestrales. Elle préparait toujours ses mémorables boulettes de viande et son couscous pour le repas de la veille du shabbat, en les épiçant tout spécialement à mode familiale.

Et elle portait le bracelet en or de sa mère tous les jours de sa vie.

Et même si le bracelet en or d'Élise avait disparu après ou peut-être avant que cette histoire ne soit écrite, la chaîne des aïeules ne serait pas interrompue. Il serait toujours possible de transmettre leur souvenir à ses deux petites-filles, ainsi qu'un autre nouveau-vieux bracelet.

Références pour l'arbre généalogique:
L'arbre généalogique et la liste complète des références sont dans la section de l'original en anglais.

AKNIN, Mimoun: *certificat de décès*
http://anom.archivesnationales.culture.gouv.fr/caomec2/osd.php?territoire=ALGERIE&acte=667547
Ce certificat de son décès, est très probablement le sien. Il a été enregistré par son beau-fils Salomon Soussan qui parlait français mais ne l'écrivait pas. La femme de Mimoun était aussi connue sous le nom de Zahra ben Kemmoun. Zahri Laïk a probablement été nommée d'après cette arrière-grand-mère.

AMSELEM, Abraham (=FREDJ AMSELLEM, Abraham) & DRAY, Rebecca (=DRAÏ, Rebecca): *certificat de mariage*
http://anom.archivesnationales.culture.gouv.fr/caomec2/osd.php?territoire=ALGERIE&acte=815187
Ils n'ont pas signé en français leur certificat de mariage civil. Seul un témoin l'a signé en français, lui-même professeur de lycée.

BEN SOUSSAN, Esther (Yéyè):
Le costume de Yéyè était rouge et brodé en or, d'après la tradition orale familiale. Voir le lien ci-dessous pour les photos d'un costume traditionnel tout à fait similaire. La première photo est celle d'une femme dont le mari, Sadia El Haïk, aurait pu être un cousin éloigné du mari de Yéyè, Sadia Laïk. Il est très probable que Nouna portait le même costume que Yéyè, pour une occasion tel qu'un mariage.
https://www.mahj.org/fr/decouvrir-collections-betsalel/meriem-kasbi-tlemcen-vers-1840-oran-1915-58801
https://www.mahj.org/fr/decouvrir-collections-betsalel/portrait-de-femme-69190

Notes :

[1] http://www.terrepromise.fr/2015/06/15/les-noms-de-famille-des-juifs-dafrique-du-nord-et-leur-origine/

[2] En espagnol, littéralement: « Qui parle maure est Maure. » Le choix de l'espagnol *moro* (maure) au lieu de *árabe* (arabe) n'est pas anodin. On parle à tort de l'invasion arabe en 711 de la péninsule ibérique. En fait les envahisseurs berbères étaient bien plus nombreux que les Arabes. « C'est pourquoi les Espagnols, pour évoquer la domination musulmane, préfèrent parler de Maures, c'est-à-dire de Maghrébins. » (Joseph Pérez, *Histoire de l'Espagne*, éditions Fayard, 1996, p. 34.)
Pour une espagnole du XVème siècle, le terme *Moro* se réfère donc principalement à ces Berbères islamisés et parlant l'arabe. Dans l'esprit de la grand-mère de Fabienne ce terme implique que les Berbères juifs arabophones sont des Maures. Jamais un Juif d'Algérie ne ce considèrerait comme un Maure. Ce terme était réservé aux musulmans. Traiter un Berbère juif de Maure, c'était jeter un doute sur sa judéité et donc sur sa compatibilité pour un mariage juif.
L'expression « Quiconque parle arabe est un Arabe » n'est pas par elle-même péjorative. Elle se retrouve dans un *hadîth*:
http://www.aibl.fr/seances-et-manifestations/coupoles-312/coupole-2015/article/quiconque-parle-arabe-est-un-arabe?lang=fr

³ Confirmant cette étymologie, Abraham Elhaïk, né à Tlemcen, Algérie, a changé son nom en Laïk en 1907. *El* représente l'article défini en Arabe. http://anom.archivesnationales.culture.gouv.fr/caomec2/osd.php?territoire=ALGERIE&acte=568550
Le nom Elhaïk appartenait apparemment aussi à une famille berbère influente, liée au roi du Maroc. (Communication personnelle du Docteur Nabil Kotby)

⁴ https://www.ynetnews.com/articles/0,7340,L-4486149,00.html
http://my.ynet.co.il/pic/news/nombres.pdf

Nouna

Élise a dû se débattre lorsqu'elle a pris la décision audacieuse de quitter son père après s'être occupé de lui et de ses frères et tenir la maison à la suite du décès de sa mère. Lors de sa décision de racheter un cabinet dentaire à Oran, elle s'est probablement sentie coupable de s'éloigner de la tradition, et de ne pas avoir rempli le rôle de femme qu'on attendait d'elle. Cependant, ses ancêtres avaient déjà été initié le changement de tradition et elle suivait simplement leur chemin, réalisant ainsi leur rêve d'intégration dans la société française.

On peut observer le changement culturel à travers les générations dans la famille d'Élise, par le biais de photographies montrant un changement de mode vestimentaire, de documents écrits d'origine civile ou religieuse, et de récits oraux.[1] La colonisation française de l'Algérie entraina la création d'un registre d'état civil à partir de 1830. Ce registre fournit des instantanés de la famille d'Élise.

Le père d'Élise a changé son prénom, Messaoud, d'origine arabe, en Prosper, son équivalent français. Les grands-parents de Messaoud étaient Messaoud et Messaouda. De toute évidence, le prénom Messaoud devait être populaire dans la famille au moment de la naissance de Prosper en 1884. 74 ans plus tard, un prénom d'origine arabe n'était plus adapté à la culture ambiante. Malgré son âge, il fit l'effort de le changer légalement en un prénom français plus conforme à son style de vie.

Prosper avait lui-même suivi la voie tracée par ses parents vers un changement culturel. Son père avait hérité de noms de Juifs expulsés d'Espagne, tandis que sa mère avait des origines berbères du sud du Maroc. A travers ce mariage « mixte » entre Juifs d'Espagne et Juifs Berbères, les deux communautés s'unissaient et perdaient leurs spécificités. Contrairement aux rivières de Babylone immortalisées dans les Psaumes (137: 1), les souvenirs tribaux d'une rivière appelée Oued Draa avaient disparu. Un nouveau récit, une nouvelle histoire étaient progressivement réécrits. Ils supplantèrent la conscience d'un passé berbère, et ont obscurci la mémoire de l'expulsion d'Espagne. Avec cette réécriture de l'histoire, Prosper construisit fièrement son identité juive française. Au point où, à la fin de la colonisation, la famille de Prosper a suivi les colons français comme les autres Juifs d'Algérie. Ils ont émigré en masse, bien que les Juifs d'origine berbère résidaient en Algérie avant l'arrivée de l'islam et des Arabes au Maghreb.[2]

À la différence de ses parents, Prosper parlait le français couramment, démontrant une meilleure intégration avec la France. Prosper était connu pour sa belle écriture manuscrite en français. Malgré tout, il avait aussi gardé ses racines espagnoles, et il parlait l'espagnol avec l'accent de Valence, selon sa petite-fille Jacqueline.

Les photographies de familles nous montrent aussi un processus similaire de sécularisation et de francisation. Dans une photographie posée, le père de Prosper portait un turban et sa mère une traditionnelle robe juive ornée. Cette robe présente une similitude frappante avec celle de Yéyè, également d'origine berbère. Prosper, lui, a été photographié jeune homme déjà vêtu d'un style français moderne.

À quoi Prosper s'attendait-il, lui qui a embrassé la culture et la langue françaises et dont la fille, Élise, élevée en Algérie, ne connaissait que l'arabe de base nécessaire pour acheter de la nourriture sur le marché local ? Dans sa rébellion, Élise ne faisait que poursuivre ses idéaux.

Le décret Crémieux a octroyé la nationalité française en 1870 aux Juifs d'Algérie. Probablement pour prouver leurs ascendance juive et donc française, les enregistrements des mariages civil et religieux de Nouna en 1846 ont été conservés dans la famille. Conformément à l'exigence encore en vigueur en France, le mariage civil a précédé le mariage religieux. La *ketouba* certifiant le mariage juif est entièrement écrite en caractères hébreux, à l'exception d'un cachet portant la mention « timbre royal » dans son coin supérieur gauche.

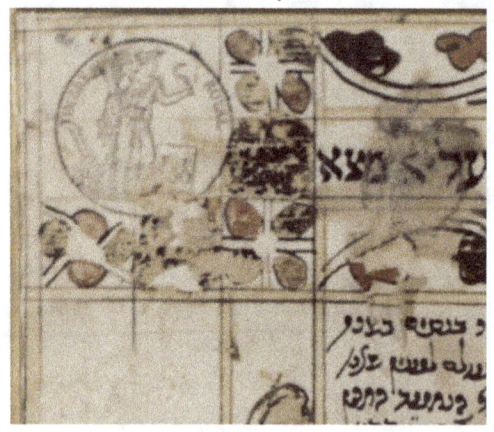

Timbre royal, d'une valeur de 50 centimes, sur la ketouba de Nouna

Le roi Louis-Philippe, le dernier roi français, a abdiqué en 1848, moins de deux ans après le mariage religieux de Nouna, le 24 mars 1846. Puisque le timbre royal n'était pas requis, on pourrait penser que la *ketouba* était plus royaliste que le roi ! En cherchant l'aval du roi de France, la *ketouba* a implicitement donné son approbation à la France à travers ce sceau. Elle l'a fait de manière plus explicite dans son texte même, en hébreu, reflétant l'identification enthousiaste avec la France de la communauté juive de l'époque.

On peut imaginer la communauté faisant pression sur le futur mari de Nouna pour qu'il augmente le remboursement de la dot en cas de divorce, afin d'arrondir et d'obtenir une somme plus importante. La *ketouba* affiche fièrement cet accord en grand caractères gras:

TROIS MILLE FRANCS BEAUX ET BONS de la monnaie de France, « qu'elle soit renforcée, Amen. » Tout lui venu en sa main et sous son autorité.

Malgré cette langue hyperbolique traditionnelle, dédiée ici à la France, en réalité, d'après l'acte civil du mariage, tout le monde ne savait pas écrire ou même parler français lors de ce mariage, et un interprète avait été requis à la mairie d'Oran pour la cérémonie civile. La voix de Nouna n'a pas été enregistrée lors de cette procédure, mais on peut imaginer que cette jeune femme de 18 ans valait l'attention d'une reine le jour de son mariage. Et le mariage a tenu bon. Salomon n'a pas divorcé Nouna. On le voit inscrire en bon époux, après 10 ans de mariage, le décès du père de Nouna. Elle mourut deux mois après lui, en 1888, après 40 ans de mariage. Qui sait, peut-être que sa vie n'avait plus de sens après qu'il fut parti.

Le processus francisation avait donc commencé bien avant la naissance d'Élise. Cependant, c'est Zahri, la mère bien-aimée d'Élise, qui a fait un saut entre les cultures. Durant sa vie la langue parlée de la famille a changé du judéo-arabe au français. Les huit enfants de Zahri portaient des prénoms français, alors que les générations précédentes utilisaient des prénoms en judéo-arabe ou en hébreu.[3] Les photographes de cette époque semblent avoir apprécié les photos de mises en scène où les gens s'habillaient tout spécialement; et les thèmes choisis pour ces images de rêve révèlent les aspirations de l'époque. Alors que la mère de Zahri, Esther, principalement connue sous son surnom de « Yéyè », se parait pour sa photo d'une magnifique robe brodée traditionnelle juive digne d'un mariage, le fantasme de Zahri était radicalement différent. On peut la voir sur sa photo, habillée comme une élégante parisienne des années 1912/1914, vêtue d'une robe longue cintrée et d'un grand chapeau à la mode. Avant son mariage, Zahri a travaillé comme couturière et come modiste et elle confectionnait des chapeaux pour un magasin de mode à Sidi-bel-Abbes. Après son mariage, elle travaillait l'après-midi dans le magasin de chaussures de son mari. Elle était aussi bien occupée à élever ses huit enfants.

Quand Élise entreprit son déménagement rebelle et laissa son père pour travailler comme dentiste dans la ville voisine, ses aïeules ont dû se porter garantes. Toutes ces femmes, à la fois du côté de sa mère et du côté de son père, pouvaient témoigner de la tension séculaire entre le passé et le présent, entre les différentes traditions juives et le désir de devenir français. Elles ont dû la soutenir et apaiser sa culpabilité.

Le récit du plateau d'Élise et la recherche d'un nouveau-vieux bracelet à Marrakech ont fait leur œuvre. Ils ont dévoilé une histoire familiale réécrite par chaque génération:
    La laïcisation du nom de famille de Zahri en « Laïk », à présent souvent interprété à tort comme une variante orthographique du mot « laïc ».
    Le souvenir flou de l'expulsion d'Espagne par des Juifs qui ont conservé leurs noms et leur accent de Valence.
    Le mode de vie perdu d'une tribu berbère au bord de la rivière Draa au sud du Maroc. Un passé si complètement éradiqué que les descendants de cette tribu n'étaient même plus conscients de leur perte; contrairement à Élise qui, malgré sa mémoire défaillante vers la fin de sa vie, se demandait encore d'où elle venait.

Comme le nouveau-vieux bracelet avec ses pyramides reliées entre elles et formant un cercle, le récit connecte les générations, les mères et les filles, le passé et le présent, l'ancien et le nouveau.

L'histoire d'Élise, Zahri, Nouna et de leurs ancêtres recrée un nouveau-vieux récit qui favorise des relations, réelles ou imaginaires, entre générations, entre Miriam et sa grand-mère Élise; entre Leah Zahri et son arrière-grand-mère Zahri Laïk et entre Zahri Laïk et son arrière-grand-mère Zahra Ben Kemmoun; et bien sûr, entre Leah, Miriam et leur père, le narrateur de cette histoire.

Notes :

[1] Jean Laloum, Le patrimoine photographique des familles juives. Un révélateur de processus d'acculturation et de sécularisation, *Questions de communication*, 2003:4, 153-185.
https://journals.openedition.org/questionsdecommunication/4952#nav
Ce processus de francisation et de sécularisation des Juifs d'Algérie a été déjà bien documenté. Voir: Joëlle Allouche-Benayoun. *La sécularisation par l'école: Filles et garçons juifs d'Algérie.* Florence Rochefort. Le Pouvoir du genre. Laïcités et religions (1905-2005), Presses Universitaires du Mirail, pp.145-159, 2007.

[2] Un documentaire décrit l'émigration de Juifs berbères de la région du Draa au Maroc: *Tinghir-Jerusalem, les échos du Mellah.* Film de Kamal Hachkar, 86 minutes, 2011; Production: Les Films d'Un Jour (France). https://www.youtube.com/watch?v=hYuTbuD9tfM

[3] Les prénoms français étaient préférés par les Juifs d'Afrique du Nord de cette génération. Voir:
Bahloul, Joëlle. Noms et prénoms juifs nord-africains, *Terrain*, 4 mars 1985, p. 62-69. https://journals.openedition.org/terrain/2872

The platter

No, said Élise. I want mine, not this one. Huguette did not understand why she was so stubborn. Huguette, her sister-in-law, had found Élise a copper platter similar to the one that Zahri, Élise's mother, had set aside in preparation for her wedding: three copper platters, one for each of her three daughters. The two oldest daughters, Fernande and Yvonne received their intended wedding gift. Unfortunately, Zahri had passed away before Élise's wedding and never had a chance to give it to her. Lison, as Élise was known, lost her copper platter. It was an injustice which had no monetary value. It was a link to her beloved mother, a reminder of a mother's love, a mother who went much too early. A mother whose black and white picture had always been on the piano in Élise's modest apartment in Paris, all those years, until Élise moved to a more grand apartment with the same piano and the same picture on top, until she moved to a room in a home without her piano, but still with the same picture, until she would wonder where she, Élise, came from.

Nevertheless, Lison had a reminder of her mother. She had her gold bracelet. A bracelet she would always wear. A simple but beautiful bracelet with a row of small square pyramids protruding on the outside, encircling the wrist. A strange design, at the same time ancient and modern, linking generations of women. Her mother or grandmother used to wear several bracelets at the same time, and each daughter must have gotten one. Lison, was especially attached to it. Her initial was engraved, an L with flourishes, interrupting the circle of pyramids, a modern adaptation for an antique piece of jewelry. Zahri must have gotten it from her own mother, Esther, probably as a wedding gift, for her dowry. It would have most certainly accompanied a copper platter, perpetuating the chain of mothers, from ancestors to daughters, a matrilineal transmission of genetic cultural heritage along with their mitochondrial DNA.

Who had Élise's copper platter? Micheline, her sister-in-law had taken it after her marriage, the same year but before Élise's wedding. Until then the platter had been left alone waiting for the third daughter, Élise, to get married. Élise must have not been there to claim it at that time. And then Micheline's husband also passed away, and Micheline held on to the heirloom, displaying it proudly for at least 30 years in her home, and would not give back her own memory. For her, Élise's coveted copper platter was a competitive narrative, a fight for the past which affected the present. And then Micheline herself passed away, and who knows among her children who inherited Lison's copper platter. Lison is not in this world to claim it anymore. But the chain, the chain, the chain of mothers is still holding, as long as their memories are alive and Élise's granddaughters, Leah Zahri (named after Élise's mother) and Miriam, are ready to pass on their heritage.[38]

Three platters. Three daughters. Fernande, Yvonne, and Élise. Was there a hidden message retrievable only if the three platters were once put together, like the three parchments belonging to the three brothers in Tintin's *Secret of the Licorne*? Was Zahri, along with all the female ancestors, still hoping that the tradition would be continued and that they would be remembered? Were Zahri and Élise and all the women before them trying to connect to Leah Zahri and Miriam?

The three daughters had already joined their mother, Zahri, in the next world, reunited at last. Fernande's oldest daughter would have inherited the copper platter. It was passed down in her family, and could be retrieved. Yvonne, Zahri's second

---

[38] The first names of Élise's granddaughters were changed for this story.

daughter, lived in Toulon in the south of France at the end of her life, and she also displayed her platter proudly. It was hung prominently on the wall, above the sofa in her lovely small apartment, a sparkling clean home, with a terrace and a view to the Mediterranean Sea. Yvonne loved to talk. She was the only one who could silence her younger sister Lison. Yvonne would apply the Midrash to her mother Zahri, explaining how Élie the prophet would bless a welcoming home, and describing how Zahri's home was open to guests.

Yvonne and Lison told the exact same story the preparation of a holiday table for the numerous family members (the 3 sisters had also 5 brothers), with very little space between seats. Nevertheless, Zahri would ask to add another seat. "But why?" Yvonne questioned her mother, "I counted well, we don't need the extra seat." Yvonne recalled proudly what her mother answered: "If someone comes unexpectedly and doesn't see an empty seat they would feel that they were not welcome."

Yvonne also remembered her mother's response when a poor family member would come and steal some change which was in the entrance. Yvonne alerted her mother about this small theft. Zahri answered: "My daughter, I know they are stealing it. I leave the change there on purpose. Sometimes it is difficult to ask."

Yvonne's copper platter was not on her wall anymore, but tucked on top of a shelf in her daughter's living room. The memory of that platter is still here and its picture shows a very unusual chiseled design. The link to the past is not broken. Other traditions and stories have survived, at least in memory:

    The glass of water a mother would empty for good luck on the floor outside the door in the direction of a dear family member about to leave for a long time, while saying in Arabic *"trek slemme"*, "go in peace".[39]

The Passover *seder* plate, turned three times above the head of each participant at the beginning of the reading of the *hagadah*.

The golden coin (*Louis d'or*), placed on top of the couscous made with butter for the Mimouna, the feast marking the end of Passover.

The fond memory of the communal oven where Jewish families would bring their food on Friday afternoon, in order to have a warm meal on Shabbat day, and circumvent the cooking prohibition.

The sigh accompanied with the Arabic words *"Aye imeh!"* (meaning "Oh mother!"), when things were not going so well.

The last minute food preparation by the women for the break-fast of Yom Kippur when they would hear the men from the nearby synagogue singing *besha'at haneila* with renewed enthusiasm for the closing service.

The endless sharing of the homemade holiday cookies with their traditional flavor, uniting the entire family like a chain letter, from the woman who baked it down to the rest of the family and even trickling to members now far away; each one required to pass on a piece of the flavored memory to a child, a sibling, a loved one, to pass on the tradition, connecting to the past, the ancestors, the old country, down to the last crumb.

And of course, there was the bracelet. The golden bracelet of Lison marked with an ornate "*L*".

---

[39] See: https://azititou.wordpress.com/2012/06/29/le-verre-deau/

Chiseled platter which belonged to Yvonne, Zahri's daughter.

Yvonne's platter (detail)

The bracelet

Write the story, so that the story does not repeat itself. Write the story of the bracelet, so that the story of the copper platter does not repeat itself, so that the bracelet goes to its intended destiny, to its intended owner, perpetuating the chain of relationships between generations, between the living and the dead, between the ancestors and their descendants, between the mothers and the daughters, and the daughters who became themselves mothers.

One golden bracelet. Two daughters. One bracelet short. Zahri's mother was wearing many bracelets as was the custom, and their number dwindled by the generations. The golden bracelet of Lison, already marked with an L will go to the oldest granddaughter, Leah, on her wedding day, God willing. Miriam will get a new bracelet. A new-old bracelet, a new bracelet made of an old one, like the old-new country, Israel, the *Altneuland* (the Old-New Land) of Theodore Herzl, or the Old-New Synagogue of Prague, the Altneuschul.

But where to find a new bracelet like the old one?

Miriam and her father could not go to Algeria anymore, because it wasn't safe. However Sidi-Bel-Abbes and Oran are close to Morocco. The Jewish customs of western Algeria are similar to those in neighboring Morocco, and some of the ancestors clearly came from that country. The answer was in the huge souk of Marrakesh. Tucked in the midst of the scents and the colors of the spice souk, the carpet souk, the metalworking souk, the shoe souk, the potter souk, and the souk *des teinturiers* (fabric dyers), was a store with an amazing find: A shiny antique silver bracelet resembling the golden one. The storekeeper explained that the pyramids of the bracelet had originally a utilitarian function, in addition to its esthetic quality: It was used by washwomen to rub a dirty spot when attempting to clean it. And, the store-keeper added, it was Berber jewelry.

Berber jewelry? Was Élise a descendant from her mother's side of a Berber tribe converted to Judaism before Islam arrived in the Maghreb?

Miriam was so pleased with her new bracelet, especially because of the renewed connection with a past she was building, even if the uninterrupted chain of women skipped a generation, passing through her father. Here in a little shop inside the souk of Marrakesh, she found answers about the origin of her grandmother, about her own origin. Coming back from that trip in Morocco, when hearing about the Berber provenance of the family's jewelry, Danielle reported that her mother Yvonne, Élise's sister, also suspected having Berber roots, because of the Berber songs Zahri would sing to her when Yvonne was a child.

And then there were the Berber names in Élise's family. Hidden in plain view. Aknin and Laïk from her mother side, and Draï from her father side.[1]

Aknin is a diminutive from the name Akan in the Berber language, and means "little Yaakov".

Draï is a name associated with a Jewish Berber tribe from the Oued Draa, a river in southern Morocco. The oral family tradition reported by Prosper, affirms that at least a branch of his family came from Tafilalet. Tafilalet is located in the same Moroccan region called Drâa-Tafilalet. "Why are you interested in this old stuff" answered Prosper when Fabienne, his daughter-in-law inquired about his ancestors. As if to say that it was a bygone time, of which we were not particularly proud, and that it was time to turn over a new leaf: we are civilized now! Fabienne's grandmother, proud of her Spanish-Jewish origin, still spoke a Spanish from the 15th century in Tétouan. When Fabienne announced to her that she intended to marry a young man from an Arabic-speaking Jewish family, she responded with disdain: *"Quien habla moro es moro."* (He who speaks Arabic is Arabic.[2]) But when Fabienne mentioned Prosper's family, her grandmother gave her approval: "With them we can. They, at least, they are civilized." Apparently, in Tétouan, the social status of Jews of Berber origin was lower than the one of Spanish Jews. However Prosper had succeeded in blurring the Berber past of the family, to the point that Élise never mentioned Tafilalet and her tribal origin; and she probably didn't know anything about it. Without Fabienne's questions, Prosper's memory about Tafilalet would have been lost, and only the name of Draï would have survived.

The third name, Laïk, Zahri's maiden name, derived from *El Haïk*, a Berber family name.[3] Elhaïk changed his name from a clearly recognizable Arabic sounding word in the land of Islam, by making it literally more secular (*laïc* in French); while keeping a connection to the past and the structure of his former name including its final letter "k". This name change exemplifies a process of secularization (*laïcisation* in French) while still maintaining a connection with the past.

The word "El Haïk" represents a Berber garment (hâyk هايك) of Roman origin: it is a long fabric of 1.5 meters which is rolled up and held at the waist by a belt, and then picked up on the shoulders where it is maintained by a hook; by extension it corresponds in Arabic to the weaver's craft.[1] The haïk also used to be worn by Berber men like was the toga in ancient Rome, and did not necessarily cover the face. Now, the haïk is disappearing, and is mainly worn by some Muslim women who use it to cover their face like with an Islamic scarf, similar to a Niqab.

In addition to her Berber origin, Élise who spoke French and Spanish fluently had family names on her father side (Amselem and Sayag), from Jews expelled from Spain in 1492. Those names are on a published list recognizing them as being eligible for a fast track Spanish citizenship as descendants of Jews expelled from Spain.[4]

Élise, champion of secularism, fought for women's rights and despised the practice of face covering by Muslim women, because she saw it as oppressive. How ironic that Élise had a mother whose original name, Laïk, did not mean "secular" (*laïc* in French), but has been with time associated with clothes covering the faces of women!

Élise followed the path of her older brother, Roger, and became a dentist, a rare achievement for a woman in Algeria in the 1950's. Élise wanted to be a physician, but was afraid that she would not be respected as a woman, so she chose to be a dentist, thinking that she would be better accepted. However, when her mother passed away in 1949, Élise, as the youngest and unmarried daughter was expected to fill her mother's shoes and take care of the household, including her father and brothers. After a year of fulfilling that role, she realized that she was wasting her dental diploma, and that she would stay an old maid if she were to continue down that road. So, breaking the tradition, she left her father in Sidi-Bel-Abbes and bought a dental practice in Oran. Only God can imagine how guilty she must have felt to follow her own path as a woman; guilt mixed with anger toward the male religious establishment. Still breaking with tradition, she responded to a matrimonial ad (or maybe she even placed one, we will never know) and married a Jewish man living in the "métropole" as they used to call what was mainland France, who was not even from the Maghreb! Élise kept the secret of the matrimonial ad throughout her life. When asked how she met her husband across the Mediterranean Sea, she would answer with the same cryptic phrase and a smile, that it was her "secret garden".

Even when her memory faded, Élise kept being proud, and with good reason, of being a dentist. She derived great satisfaction from her dental practice in Paris even if it meant working long hours. She loved treating Arab workers from North Africa, and Blacks from former French colonies in Africa. They were her main clients, and they preferred coming to see her rather than going to the nearby state sponsored dental clinic. They must have felt a common sensibility, a different non-verbal way of interacting, like in their homes. Before returning to their country, they would insist on completing as much dental work with her as possible, because she carried the prestige of the métropole. At their return, they wanted to show that they had succeeded in France; and their smile adorned with a gold tooth would be their proof for all to see. A client even asked her once to remove a very healthy front tooth, and replace it with a gold tooth, which Élise refused to do.

Despite being born in Algeria, her skin was light, perhaps because of her Spanish ancestry. Her married name did not sound North African or Jewish, so Élise could pass as a dentist from the heartland France. She did not want to disclose that she was *de là-bas* ("from there", meaning from Algeria) because she learned that it was better not to be too obviously Jewish.

Élise, a resolutely modern and emancipated woman, did not lose her ancestral roots. She was still making her memorable *boulettes* (meatballs) and couscous for the Shabbat eve meal, spicing them in the special family way.

And she wore her mother's gold bracelet every day of her life.

Even if Élise's gold bracelet had disappeared after or maybe before this story was written, the women ancestors' chain would not be interrupted. It would still be possible to pass on their memory to both her granddaughters, along with another oldnew bracelet.

The ancestors

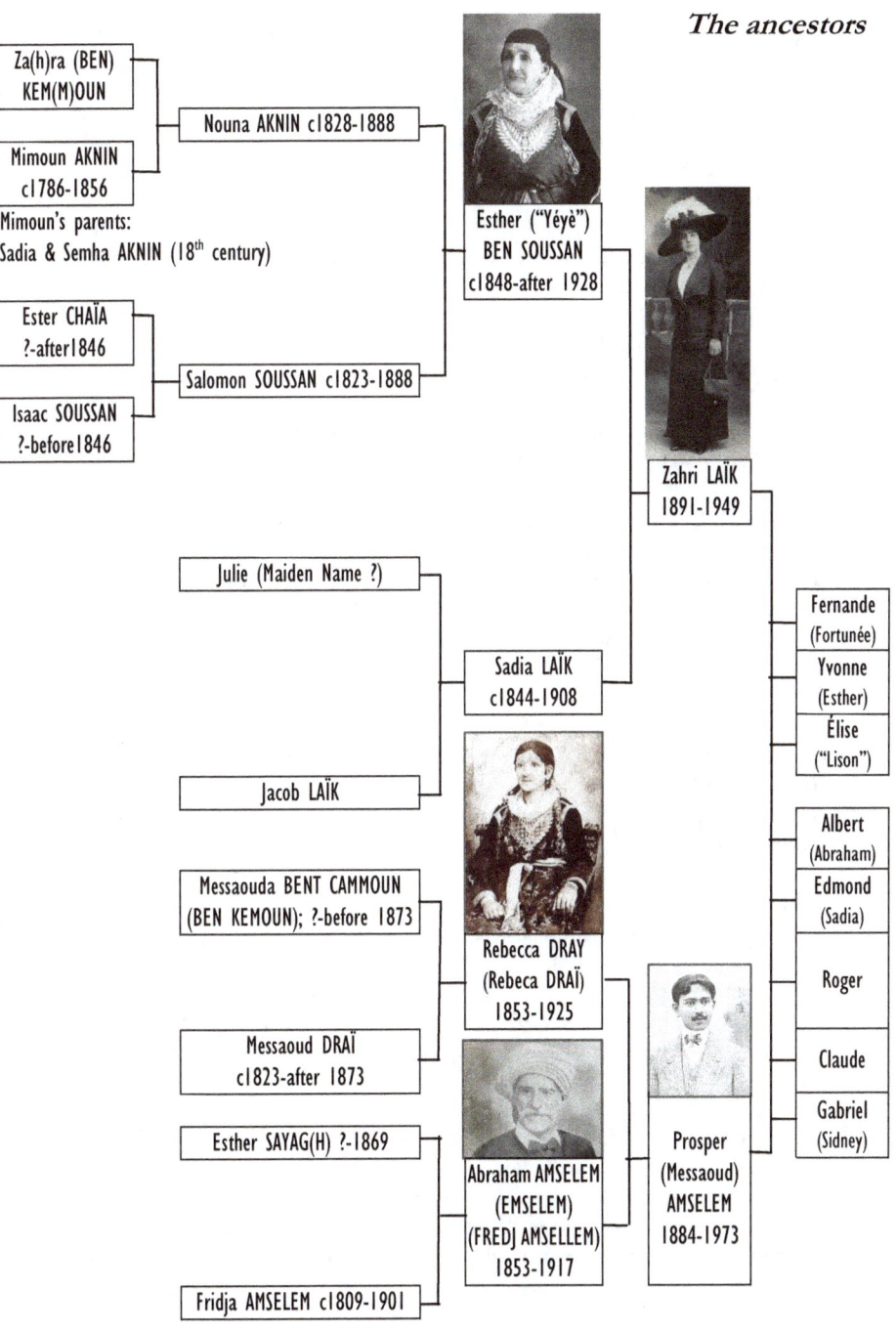

References for the genealogy tree:

AKNIN, Mimoun: *death certificate*
http://anom.archivesnationales.culture.gouv.fr/caomec2/osd.php?territoire=ALGERIE&acte=667547
This death certificate most likely belongs to him. It was registered by his son-in-law Salomon Soussan who spoke French but could not write it. Mimoun's wife was also known as Zahra ben Kemmoun. Zahri Laïk was probably named after her great-grandmother Zahra.

AKNIN, Nouna: *death certificate*
http://anom.archivesnationales.culture.gouv.fr/caomec2/osd.php?territoire=Algerie&acte=643386
https://gw.geneanet.org/pierrebenoliel?lang=en&pz=pierre+felix&nz=benoliel&ocz=0&p=nouna&n=aknin

AMSELEM, Abraham (=FREDJ AMSELLEM, Abraham) & DRAY, Rebecca (=DRAÏ, Rebecca): *marriage certificate*
http://anom.archivesnationales.culture.gouv.fr/caomec2/osd.php?territoire=ALGERIE&acte=815187
They did not sign their civil marriage certificate in French letters. Only one witness signed in French, himself a high school teacher.

AMSELEM, Fridja: *death certificate*
http://anom.archivesnationales.culture.gouv.fr/caomec2/osd.php?territoire=ALGERIE&acte=890766
https://gw.geneanet.org/pierrebenoliel?lang=en&pz=pierre+felix&nz=benoliel&ocz=0&p=fridja&n=amsalem&oc=1

AMSELEM, Prosper: *birth certificate, marriage certificate*
http://anom.archivesnationales.culture.gouv.fr/caomec2/osd.php?territoire=ALGERIE&acte=714437
http://anom.archivesnationales.culture.gouv.fr/caomec2/osd.php?territoire=ALGERIE&registre=39201 (picture number 20, at the left of the screen, not the number of the marriage certificate).

BEN SOUSSAN, Esther (Yéyè):
Yéyè's dress was red, and embroidered in gold, according to the family oral tradition. See below the link to pictures with a very similar traditional outfit. The first one belongs to a woman whose husband, Sadia El Haïk, may have been related to Yéyè's husband, Sadia Laïk. It is very likely that Nouna was wearing an outfit like Yéyè's, for a festive occasion like a wedding.

https://www.mahj.org/fr/decouvrir-collections-betsalel/meriem-kasbi-tlemcen-vers-1840-oran-1915-58801
https://www.mahj.org/fr/decouvrir-collections-betsalel/portrait-de-femme-69190

DRAÏ, Salomon (Rebecca Dray's brother): *marriage and death certificates*
http://anom.archivesnationales.culture.gouv.fr/caomec2/osd.php?territoire=ALGERIE&acte=815027
http://anom.archivesnationales.culture.gouv.fr/caomec2/osd.php?territoire=ALGERIE&acte=880815

LAÏK, Zahri: *birth certificate*
http://anom.archivesnationales.culture.gouv.fr/caomec2/osd.php?territoire=ALGERIE&acte=545250

SAYAGH, Esther (=SAYAG, Ester; SAÏAG, Ester):
Her name, lost in the family tradition, was found in her son's marriage certificate.
https://gw.geneanet.org/pierrebenoliel?lang=en&pz=pierre+felix&nz=benoliel&ocz=0&p=ester&n=saiag

SOUSSAN, Salomon (=Salomon BENSOUSSAN): *death certificate*
http://anom.archivesnationales.culture.gouv.fr/caomec2/osd.php?territoire=ALGERIE&acte=642562

Notes:

[1] http://www.terrepromise.fr/2015/06/15/les-noms-de-famille-des-juifs-dafrique-du-nord-et-leur-origine/

[2] In Spanish, literally "He who speaks Moor is Moor." The choice of the Spanish *moro* (Moor) instead of *árabe* (Arabic) is significant. We describe wrongly the invasion of Spain in 711 as being Arabic. In fact, the Berber invaders were much more numerous than the Arabs. "This is why the Spaniards, when discussing the Muslim domination, prefer to talk about Moors, which means from the Maghreb." (Joseph Pérez, Histoire de l'Espagne, éditions Fayard, 1996, p. 34.) For a Spaniard in the 15th century, the term *moro* refers mainly to Arabic-speaking Islamized Berbers. In the mind of Fabienne's grandmother, this term implies that the Arabic-speaking Jewish Berbers are Moors. Never would an Algerian Jew call himself Moor. This denomination was reserved for the Muslims. To call someone a Moor was to cast a doubt over his Jewishness, and therefore

over his appropriateness for a Jewish wedding. The expression "He who speaks Arabic is Arab" is not by itself pejorative. We find it in a *hadîth*: http://www.aibl.fr/seances-et-manifestations/coupoles-312/coupole-2015/article/quiconque-parle-arabe-est-un-arabe?lang=fr

[3] Confirming this etymology, Abraham Elhaïk, born nearby in Tlemcen, Algeria, changed his last name legally to Laïk in 1907. *El* is the Arabic definite article.
http://anom.archivesnationales.culture.gouv.fr/caomec2/osd.php?territoire=ALGERIE&acte=568550 The name Elhaïk also belongs to an influential Berber family well connected to the king of Morocco. (Personal communication from Doctor Nabil Kotby)

[4] https://www.ynetnews.com/articles/0,7340,L-4486149,00.html
http://my.ynet.co.il/pic/news/nombres.pdf

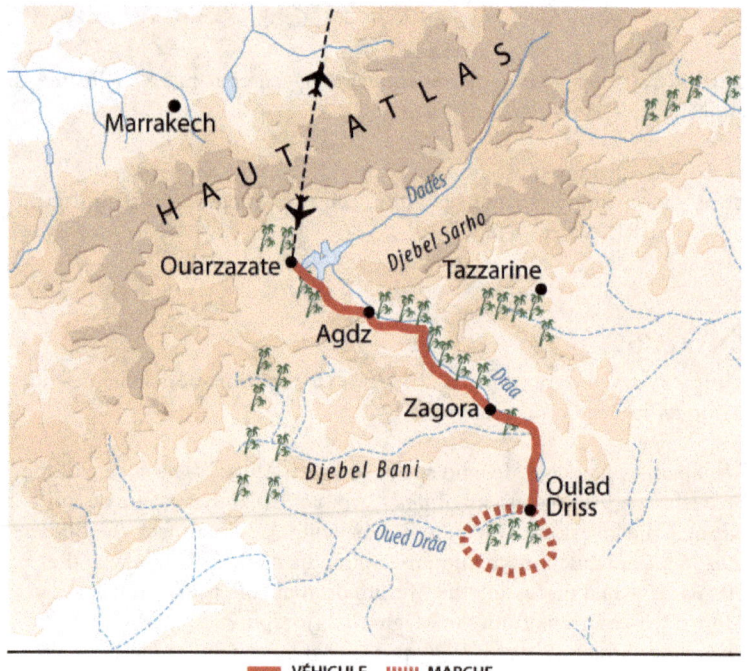

The Draa River
https://www.huwans-clubaventure.fr/voyage/voyage-trek-et-randonnee/maroc/mdra

The Oued (river) Draa starts from the region of Ouarzazate down to the Atlantic Ocean. The family name Draï is associated with a Jewish Berber tribe from that river. A hypothetical trek from the Oued Draa starting in Zagora, up north to Sidi-Bel-Abbes, would take currently 18 ½ hours by car according to Google Map. It would pass by Tinghir (see page 250), and Tafilalt, an ancestral place for Prosper's family.

Berber bracelet, Morocco.

Nouna

Élise must have struggled when she made the bold move of leaving her father after taking care of him and her brothers and running the household for the year following her mother's death. After her decision to buy a dental practice in Oran, she probably felt guilty for not following her expected woman's role, and departing from tradition. However, her ancestors had already initiated the change in tradition, and she only followed their path of change, fulfilling their dream of integration with the French society.

We can observe the culture change across generations within Élise's family, by using photographs displaying change in fashion, written documents from civil or religious origin, and oral narratives[1]. The French colonization of Algeria led to the creation of a civil registry of birth, marriage, and death starting in 1830. This registry provides snapshots of Élise's family.

Élise's father changed his first name, Messaoud, of Arabic origin, into Prosper, its French equivalent. Messaoud's grandparents were Messaoud and Messaouda. Clearly, the first name Messaoud must have been popular in the family at the time of Prosper's birth in 1884. 74 years later, an Arabic first name no longer fit the changing culture. Despite his age and the effort it required, Messaoud legally changed his name to a French first name more congruent with his lifestyle.

Prosper had himself followed his parents' path of culture change. His father inherited names of Jews expelled from Spain, while his mother had Berber origins from the south of Morocco. Through this "mixed" marriage between Spanish Jews and Berber Jews, the two communities merged and lost their distinctive characteristics. Unlike the memories of the Babylon River, immortalized in the Psalms (137:1), the tribal memories of a river called Oued Draa had disappeared. A new narrative, a new history were progressively rewritten. They almost erased the consciousness of a Berber past, and faded the memory of the expulsion from Spain. With this rewriting of history, Prosper proudly built his French Jewish identity to the extent that, when the French colonization ended, Prosper's family followed the French settlers along with the rest of the Algerian Jewry. They emigrated en masse, even though the Jews of Berber origin settled in Algeria before the arrival of Islam and the Arabs in the Maghreb.[2]

Prosper was proficient in French, unlike his parents, demonstrating a greater integration with France. He was known for his beautiful handwriting in French. Nevertheless, he also kept his Spanish heritage. He spoke Spanish with a Valencian accent, according to his granddaughter Jacqueline.

The family photographs show a similar process of secularization and westernization. In a posed picture, Prosper's father wore a turban and his mother a traditional Jewish ornate robe. That robe bears a striking similarity to one worn by Yéyè, also of Berber origin. Prosper, however, was photographed as a young man, already dressed in a modern French style.

What did Prosper expect, he who embraced the French culture and language, and whose daughter Élise, raised in Algeria, knew only the basic Arabic necessary to buy food at the local market? In her rebellion, Élise was just pursuing his ideals.

The Crémieux Decree of 1870 gave French nationality to the Jews in Algeria. Presumably, in order to prove their Jewish and therefore French credentials, the civil and religious records of Nouna's marriage in 1846 were kept in the family.

Consistent with the requirement still current in France, the civil wedding preceded the religious one. The *ketuba* which certifies the Jewish wedding is written entirely in Hebrew characters except for the *timbre royal* (royal seal) proudly displayed on its upper left corner.

"Timbre royal" (royal seal), with a 50 cent value, on Nouna's ketuba

King Louis-Philippe, the last French king, abdicated in 1848, less than two years after Nouna's religious wedding. Since the royal seal was not required, what comes to mind is the French expression *"plus royaliste que le roi"* ("more royalist than the king"). By seeking Louis-Philippe's seal of approval, the endorsement of the French king, the *ketuba* implicitly endorsed France. It did so more explicitly within the core of its Hebrew text, reflecting the enthusiastic identification with France by the Jewish community of the time.

We can imagine the community pressuring Nouna's future husband to augment the reimbursement of the dowry in case of divorce, by rounding up in order to achieve a larger sum. The *ketuba* proudly displays this agreement in large and bold characters:

> **THREE THOUSAND FRANCS BEAUTIFUL AND GOOD** from the money of France, "may she be reinforced, Amen." All came by her hand and under her authority.

Despite this traditional hyperbolic language, here dedicated to France, not everyone could write or even speak French at that wedding. According to the civil marriage certificate, an interpreter had been required at Oran's city hall for that civil ceremony. Nouna's voice has not been recorded in those proceedings but we could imagine that this young woman of 18 was worth the attention of a queen on her marriage day. And the marriage did hold. Salomon did not divorce Nouna. We see him reporting to the city hall, as a good husband, the death of Nouna's father, 10 years into their marriage. Remarkably, she died only 2 months after him, in 1888, after 40 years of marriage. Who knows, maybe her life did not make sense after he was gone.

The processes of becoming more culturally French had therefore started well before Élise was born. However, it is Élise's beloved mother, Zahri, who made a cultural jump. During Zahri's lifetime the spoken language of the family was switched from Judeo-Arabic to French. The eight children of Zahri's had French first names, while the previous generations used only Judeo-Arabic or Hebrew first names.[3] The photographers of the time seem to have enjoyed a staged setting where people played dress up, and the themes chosen for those fantasy tableaux reveal the aspirations of the time. While Zahri's mother, Esther, known mainly by her nickname "Yéyè", adorns herself for her picture with her magnificent traditional Jewish embroidered robe suited for a wedding, Zahri's fantasy was dramatically different. In her picture, she dressed like an elegant Parisian woman around 1912/1914 wearing a fitted long dress and a large fashionable hat. Before her marriage, Zahri worked as a seamstress and a hat designer (*modiste* in French) in a fashionable store of Sidi-bel-Abbes. After her marriage, she worked part-time at her husband's shoe store. She was also very busy raising her eight children.

So, when Élise made her rebellious move and left her father in order to work as a dentist in the city nearby, she had many ancestors to vouch for her. All those women, both from her mother and her father's side, could testify to the long standing tension between the past and the present, between the different Jewish traditions and the aspirations of becoming French. They must have supported her and eased her guilt.

The story of Élise's platter, and the search for an oldnew bracelet in Marrakech worked their magic. They unveiled a family history rewritten by each generation:

    The secularization of Zahri's last name, Laïk, now often misinterpreted as being a spelling variant of the word *"laïc"* (meaning "secular" in French).

    The blurred recollection of the expulsion from Spain by Jews who still kept their names and their accent from Valencia.

    The lost lifestyle of a Berber tribe along the river Draa in the south of Morocco. A past erased so completely that the descendants of that tribe were not even aware of their loss; unlike Élise who still wondered where she came from towards the end of her life, despite her fading memory.

Like the oldnew bracelet with its pyramids linked together in circle, the story binds the generations, the mothers and the daughters, the past and the present, the old and the new.

The story of Élise, Zahri, Nouna and their ancestors recreates an oldnew narrative which fosters relationships, real or imagined, between generations, between Miriam and her grandmother Élise; between Leah Zahri and her great-grandmother Zahri Laïk, and between Zahri Laïk and her own great-grandmother Zahra Ben Kemmoun; and, of course, between Leah, Miriam and their father, the narrator of this story.

Notes:

[1] Jean Laloum. Le patrimoine photographique des familles juives. Un révélateur de processus d'acculturation et de sécularisation, *Questions de communication*, 2003:4, 153-185.
https://journals.openedition.org/questionsdecommunication/4952#nav
This process of French integration and secularization of the Jews in Algeria has been well documented. See: Joëlle Allouche-Benayoun. *La sécularisation par l'école: Filles et garçons juifs d'Algérie*. Florence Rochefort. Le Pouvoir du genre. Laïcités et religions (1905-2005), Presses Universitaires du Mirail, pp.145-159, 2007.

[2] A documentary describes the emigration of Berber Jews from the Draa region in nearby Morocco: *Tinghir-Jerusalem, les échos du Mellah*. Movie by Kamal Hachkar, 86 minutes, 2011; Production: Les Films d'Un Jour (France). https://www.youtube.com/watch?v=hYuTbuD9tfM

[3] French first names were preferred for that generation of Jews in North Africa. See:
Bahloul, Joëlle. Noms et prénoms juifs nord-africains, *Terrain*, 4 mars 1985, p. 62-69. https://journals.openedition.org/terrain/2872

Ketuba of Nouna Aknin, Zahri's granddaughter, on March 24, 1846.

Esther (Yéyè) Ben Soussan (c1848-after 1928), daughter of Nouna. This traditional Jewish dress was red, embroidered in gold.

Yéyè's daughter, Zahri Laïk (1891-1949), around 1912/1914. She was probably named after her great-grandmother Zahra ben Kemmoun. Their first name was common to both Jews and Muslims. This picture reveals the rapid westernization of the generation right after Yéyè.

Rebecca Dray (1853-1925), mother of Prosper Amselem, dressed in a traditional Jewish dress, resembling Yéyè's.

Abraham Amselem (1853-1917) and Rebecca Draï.

Prosper Amselem (1884-1973), son of Abraham and Rebecca. On the left Prosper, 18, in 1902, is dressed as a fashionable young man of his time, not wearing the turban of his father. Those pictures highlight the rapid culture change embraced by both Prosper and his wife Zahri.

Forever ephemeral

We will catch up the time together
With the lasso which removes a polyp
Adding years to your life.

With the tattoo visible on a chest
Guiding radiation therapy
Or hidden inside a colon
Marking a removed tumor.

We will catch the time
My love
We will use it to build the gorgeous
Chateau of our relationship
A sand castle
Forever ephemeral
Absolutely stunning
Like life and death

We will catch the time
With those who have no more time
With our mothers and their mothers
With those who built us and made us
With those we build and make

We will catch the time
With God and our ancestors
Who made us to their image
Who we make to our image
So to speak

We will catch the time
My love
Even after the time. *New York, October 23, 2018*

The scrum (La mêlée)

Original in French 261
English translation 263

La mêlée

Tous en rond, comme dans une mêlée de rugby, la tête baissée, les bras étendus sur les épaules des autres, les mains tâtonnant se posant sur une tête, puis sur une autre, parfois sur une autre main, celle de l'autre grand-père, répartissant leur temps équitablement parmi les têtes, pour transférer la bénédiction des grands-parents aux enfants et aux petits enfants, les *talits* couvrant chaque tête, même celle d'une petite fille dans les bras de son père, la seule à se permettre de jeter un regard par-dessus la mêlée, la seule parmi ces pères, ces frères, ces frères des pères, ces pères des pères, unis pour un moment précieux, écoutant le chantre égrainant mot par mot l'ancestrale bénédiction sacerdotale, chaque mot enrobé d'une mélopée orientale, chaque mot répété avec la même mélodie par l'unique Cohen de la congrégation, ses bras étendus en avant et recouverts par un long *talit*, voilant la présence de Dieu concentrée entre ses doigts, conduisant la bénédiction divine, la multipliant à travers toute la congrégation, vers tous les groupes de têtes baissées sous leur *talit*, agglutinés par familles, incluant aussi les têtes isolées, unissant toute la communauté comme une grande famille, incluant les ancêtres, passant le flux divin à travers les mains tâtonnantes des pères et des grands-pères.

New York, le 13 janvier 2019

The scrum

All in one circle, as in a rugby scrum, head down, arms extended on the shoulders of others, fumbling hands landing on one head, then on another, sometimes on another hand, that of the other grandfather, dividing their time equitably among the heads, to transfer the blessing of grandparents to children and grandchildren, the *talits* covering each head, even that of a little girl in the arms of her father, the only one daring to cast a glance over the scrum, the only one among these fathers, these brothers, these fathers' brothers, these fathers' fathers, united for a precious moment, listening to the cantor reciting word by word the ancestral priestly blessing, each word wrapped in an oriental chant, each word repeated with the same melody by the congregation's unique Cohen, his arms extended forward and covered by a long *talit*, veiling the presence of God concentrated between his fingers, leading the divine blessing, multiplying it throughout the congregation, to all the groups of heads lowered under their *talit*, clustered by families, also including the isolated heads, uniting the whole community as a great family, connecting them with the ancestors, passing the divine flow through the fumbling hands of the fathers and grandfathers.

New York, January 13, 2019
Translated from the original in French

Afterword
267-270

Afterword
The silence of the past

By William S. Cohen

What is the transmission of an heirloom, of the traditions, of an identity? This heritage comes from the family, the ancestors, and from the community. The identified community from where the tradition is being transmitted is changing, and is being actively reconstructed by its new members. It can evolve from a Judaized Berber tribe, into a mixed Berber-Spanish Jewish community in Morocco and then in Algeria, and later on into a French Sephardic Jewish community of Algerian origin. It could evolve further in different directions.

In each generation the subtle or even drastic changes are seen as a continuation from the past, not as a total break from it. There is an attachment to the old time, an appreciation, a sometime ambivalent love and respect to the parents and the ancestors. The new generation does not want to cut itself off completely from the olden days. The changes are included in the new identity and reconciled with a different past, reconstructing it, through the generations.

The transmission of a changing history does not necessarily go smoothly. There may be bumps, conflicts, ambiguity, regrets, and nostalgia.

Two narratives describing widely different families, ***Just a brunch*** and ***The oldnew bracelet*** express a similar reticence in transmitting the past. In ***Just a brunch***, the narrator hesitates in telling the story of Tamás's sacrifice, and questions what a boy who has friends and plays video games has to do with the ancient history of his great uncle's bravery during the holocaust. The past had been almost obliterated. There was a thick silence about the holocaust in this family, and if not for the testimonial pages at Yad Vashem that history would have been lost. The silence about that painful past persisted for at least 25 years after the war, between Tamás's mother and his brother. They had learned separately about Tamás's memorial plaque and never mentioned it to each other. Maybe Tamás's surviving brother did not even know that his own grandmother perished in Auschwitz at the age of 91. And if he knew, he never mentioned it to his own family during his entire life. Now the pain is dulled, and even the remaining Holocaust survivors are more ready to talk about their experience.

In **The oldnew bracelet**, Prosper is also uncomfortable talking about the past of his family, and of his Berber origins. When asked about his ancestors from Tafilalet, he had the same reluctance and asked why anyone would be interested in this "old stuff". He was wrong, since now we are interested. However, the past was then threatening a change into a future perceived as more "civilized". The colonialist view of a "civilized" people (the French or the Spanish) versus the "savages" (the Berbers) had been integrated and incorporated into Prosper's own worldview. That colonialist view was also found among Jews themselves: Spanish Jews toward Jews of Berber origin; and Jews from mainland France (the Métropole) toward Jews in Algeria. Élise never mentioned a Berber past to her descendants, and maybe she herself had never been aware of it.

In our days, a Berber past is no longer threatening the identity of Jews living in France. The opposite: it adds a certain exotic touch of orientalism, and therefore it is now an acceptable past to uncover. Exotic touch is not the correct word. It may be correct for generations further removed from that history. However the narrative of **The oldnew bracelet** shows a deeper connection with that past, and with a story still worth transmitting.

In *Just a brunch*, like in *The oldnew bracelet*, the need for transmitting the memory overcomes the reluctance about reminiscing the past. The story is being told reluctantly in *Just a brunch*, despite a poetic warning linking the recent past with the ancient biblical story of the binding of Isaac.

In *The oldnew bracelet*, the narrative first focuses on Élise's conflict between being a modern professional and a traditional woman. The story highlights a quest for change while maintaining links with the past: the traditions and the heirlooms still cherished in the family, the name keeping intact the origin of the tribe (Draï); or the names still maintaining a link to the past even if the original names were changed (El Haïk into Laïk, Messaoud into Prosper).

This struggle of the previous generations does not leave us indifferent. The royal seal of Nouna's *ketubah* and the large fashionable hat of her granddaughter Zahri symbolize their conflicted heritage. Their struggle touches us, and raises the contemporary question of transmission to the next generation. Our struggle is still the same as for the ancestors of Élise and Tamás: what to pass on, and what to leave within the silence of the past.

In the last text, *The scrum (La mêlée)*, the narrator/observer sincerely cares about the congregants listening to the priestly blessing in a Sephardic synagogue. It may seem ironic and sacrilegious to believe that the divine flow could pass through the grandfathers' fumbling hands alternating over the heads of their children. The grandfathers are piling up their hands over the same head, as if the presence of a presumably infinite God could be divided, added and multiplied. The grandfathers' faith is not so naïve after all. Their transmission of the ancestral blessing is described as meaningful, despite a certain distance by the narrator. When looking at them with detachment, rituals may seem meaningless in the beginning, like during the mourning ceremony at the Veteran Memorial in **In a cloud of smoke**, or while singing *La Marseillaise* with an amused enthusiasm in **Let's go children**. On the surface, the rituals, and life, may look as absurd as the little artificial red flower in **In a cloud of smoke**, or the two folding stools placed at a calculated distance in **Lena**, or the oversized hat of Zahri Laïk. However, the narrator involved in the rituals appreciates their meaning, while struggling with the irony of the situation. As in **New in town** and its fear of the exterminator, even the most unspeakable text, **Just a brunch**, has this sense of gentle irony, with its Holocaust story literally sandwiched within a brunch story.

This uneasy attitude combining detachment and involvement does not detract from the gravity of the event or of life in general. There is still space to find meaning in relationships, even within this conflicted approach. In a way, the last sentence, which composes the entire text of **The scrum (La mêlée)**, is a metaphor for the entire book. It ends with a small (and in this case hopeful) slice of life, until another slice with another direction comes and covers its last words.

January 20, 2018

About the author

If you really want to hear about it, the first thing you'll probably want to know is where I was born, and what my childhood was like, and how my parents were occupied and all before they had me, but I don't feel like going into it, if you want to know the truth. All I can tell you is about that book I loved as a child. I must have read it a thousand times, no kidding. I did not know English then, so I read it in French: "L'Attrape Cœurs", it was called. I could not find the book when I finally moved all my stuff from the storage in Paris. I don't know what happened to it. You don't understand, it was a pretty important book for me, this boy lost in New York and wondering about where the ducks in Central Park would go in the freezing winter. Even now, I cannot figure it out. Maybe you can? And when he fell in love with a young nun in a long dress and a blue marine sweater. Maybe that's not exactly like that in the book, hey I lost the book OK, but it was something like that. No you don't have to be a nun and all, but I remember that one who was so nice with a visibly mentally challenged guy at the Jewish Museum. I did not talk to her then, it was many years ago, and she was not a nun, so you see you don't have to be a nun, I never said that.

www.ingramcontent.com/pod-product-compliance
Lightning Source LLC
Chambersburg PA
CBHW071304110526
44591CB00010B/772